The
HIDDEN GOSPEL

PRAISE FOR NEIL DOUGLAS-KLOTZ'S
THE HIDDEN GOSPEL

Neil Douglas-Klotz's scholarly work on the spirituality of the Aramaic Jesus brings a unique Middle Eastern perspective to the larger questions of our spiritual life and faith. The richness of the Aramaic worldview and an emphasis on spiritual practice make this book both inspirational and a profoundly practical guide for spiritual seekers.

In his study of the Aramaic Jesus, the author looks at various themes expressed in the words and stories of Jesus, not to determine their validity, but rather to uncover their depth and their power to move us "to search for our own souls." Themes such as breath, holiness, light, Sophia, and love become doorways to a fresh, deep, multilayered interpretation of Yeshua, *the native Middle Eastern man who has so influenced Western civilization for so long. Many of Neil's spiritual insights are brilliant; many are guides to an authentic practice of spirituality.*

What I most appreciate is the ease with which Neil moves back and forth from his scholarly explanations of the texts to meditation practices, body prayers, and poetic interpretations. Those who read this book will find a view of Jesus as a Middle Eastern mystic and teacher full of heart, sweetness, and wisdom!

—Marlene De Nardo, cochair of The Naropa Institute's Master's
Program in Creation Spirituality, Oakland, California

The
HIDDEN GOSPEL
—

Decoding the Spiritual Message of
the Aramaic Jesus

NEIL DOUGLAS-KLOTZ

A publication supported by
THE KERN FOUNDATION

Quest Books
Theosophical Publishing House

Wheaton, Illinois ◆ Chennai (Madras), India

The Theosophical Publishing House
P.O. Box 270
Wheaton, IL 60189-0270

A publication of the Theosophical Publishing House,
a department of the Theosophical Society in America

Cover and text design and typesetting by Beth Hansen-Winter

First Quest Hardcover Edition 1999
First Quest Paperback Edition 2001
Quest Paperback ISBN 0-8356-0795-x

The Library of Congress has cataloged the Quest hardcover edition as follows:

Douglas-Klotz, Neil.
    The hidden Gospel: decoding the spiritual message of the Aramaic Jesus /
    Neil Douglas-Klotz. — 1st Quest ed.
        p.   cm.
    Includes bibliographical references and index.
    ISBN 0-8356-0780-1
    1. Jesus Christ—Words.   2. Bible.   N.T.   Gospels—Criticism, interpreta-
    tion, etc.   3. Jesus Christ—Language.   4. Aramaic language—Religious
    aspects—Christianity.   I. Title.
BT306.D68   1999
226'.066—dc21   99-28524
                                                                    CIP

        5   4   3   *   04   05   06

Printed in the United States of America

For my mother,

FRIEDA R. KLOTZ,

who continues to teach the many faces of love.

CONTENTS

Introduction

"EVERY GOOD TREE BRINGETH FORTH GOOD FRUIT, BUT A COR-
RUPT TREE BRINGETH FORTH EVIL FRUIT" (MATTHEW 7:17).
WHEN OR IF JESUS SPOKE THOSE WORDS, HE SPOKE THEM
in a Middle Eastern language, Aramaic. In Aramaic and in all the
Semitic languages, the word for "good" primarily means ripe, and the
word for "corrupt" or "evil" primarily means unripe. When heard with
Aramaic ears, those words might sound more like this:

> "A ripe tree brings forth ripe fruit, an unripe tree brings forth
> unripe fruit."

This makes a world of difference. The tree is not morally bad, but
rather unripe: this is not the right time and place for it to bear. The
saying gives an example from nature. Rather than imposing an external
standard of goodness, the lesson has to do with time and place, setting
and circumstance, health and disease.

Likewise, whenever a saying of Jesus refers to spirit, we must remember that he would have used an Aramaic or Hebrew word. In both
of these languages, the same word stands for spirit, breath, air, and
wind. So "Holy Spirit" must also be "Holy Breath." The duality of spirit
and body, which we often take for granted in our Western languages,
falls away. If Jesus made the famous statement about speaking or sin-
ning against the Holy Spirit (for instance, in Luke 12:10), then somehow the Middle Eastern concept of breath is also involved.

The Hidden Gospel explores these simple yet radical differences
that reveal the spirituality behind the sayings of Jesus from a Middle
Eastern viewpoint. The differences stem from the nature of Middle Eastern languages themselves as well as the worldview behind them, that is,

1

the ways in which they divide and make sense of reality. The book also invites the reader to participate in the wisdom revealed by this approach as a direct, personal experience.

ANOTHER WORLD

The German philosopher Ludwig Wittgenstein once said, "The limits of my language are the limits of my world." This especially holds true for the translation and interpretation of the words of Jesus. For one thing, Middle Eastern languages allow for many different interpretations, and even different literal translations, of the words of a prophet or mystic.

If I were writing about the words of Moses or Isaiah, a Jewish audience would easily understand what I am doing in this book as *midrash*, a type of spiritual translation-interpretation that uses the possible meanings of Hebrew words as a basis for contemplation, devotion, and spiritual practice. In *midrash* one attempts through contemplation to make a scriptural passage or a saying of a holy person into a living experience that can meet the challenges of the present. Likewise, most Sufi Muslims would understand my efforts as *tawil*, a style of translation-interpretation that again considers the possible multiple meanings of a sacred text in order to cultivate wisdom for one's everyday life. As we shall explore later, in both traditions each person is free to do this interpretation in her or his own way.

In the Christian Church, especially as it evolved in the West, it became more important to determine what Jesus represented as Christ or Messiah than to look at his sayings in a Middle Eastern sense. In addition, up until the last fifty years, most Western Christian churches blamed the people they identified with "the Jews" of the Gospels for the death of Jesus. So for the Western Christian church at least, facing the question of Jesus' own Jewishness was definitely off the agenda.

Meanwhile, in scholarly circles over the past hundred years, researchers have been looking at Western textual or historical evidence for who Jesus was and what he said. In some extreme viewpoints, the factual existence of Jesus was considered a myth and was presumed to have no reality outside the text. In others, presuppositions about the nature of early Christianity prejudiced the opinions of scholars about which strands of text were the oldest and so the most historically accurate. In addition, since the primary Western and Orthodox church texts were in Greek, scholars saw no point in looking at Aramaic or Hebrew versions. To do so would have underlined Jesus' Jewishness. Most often, scholars interpreted Jesus according to Greek or Hellenistic influences of his time, rather than Middle Eastern ones. The "historical Jesus" emerged as a multitude of conflicting figures, varying according to the disposition of the scholar and the facts she or he selected.

Over the past generation, much of this has changed. There has been a concerted effort in some quarters of the Christian church to review and reinterpret the sections of the Gospels (particularly in John) that seem to demonize the people called "the Jews." One Christian scholar has made a convincing case that one cannot even speak of distinct groups called Christians or Jews in the biblical era.[1] As we shall see, the earliest so-called Jesus movements represented a multiplicity of practices and beliefs. The same was true for what we call Judaism, which also did not begin to take the organized shape we recognize today until after the destruction of the Jerusalem Temple in 70 CE. So the word translated as "Jews" in the Gospels should more accurately be translated "Judaeans"— the inhabitants of the area called Judaea by the Romans.

Even in the ten years since I published *Prayers from the Cosmos*, an interpretive translation of Jesus' sayings from an Aramaic viewpoint, there has been increasing acknowledgment by biblical scholars that the most appropriate background against which to view all early Jesus movements is one that could be called Jewish—or really, Middle Eastern. For instance, many scholars now consider that the Gospel of Thomas reflects a type of early Jewish Christian spirituality rather than a later, corrupted form of "orthodox" Christianity.[2] In addition, discussions about spirituality—the experience of the sacred—have entered scholarly and religious circles in a much larger way. As *Prayers of the Cosmos* is in keeping with these views, it has enjoyed phenomenal success world-wide. A major Protestant denomination even included parts of the book in its training handbook for ministers to broaden their perspectives on the spirituality of the Lord's Prayer.

Scholars have also acknowledged in recent years that early Christian roots not only reach back to Jewish spirituality but also extend forward in time into Islam. According to Christian scholar Hans Küng and others, some of the earliest views of Jesus (for instance, Jesus as the adopted rather than the exclusive "son of God") were preserved in early Islam. In this sense, Küng has written that Islam poses a challenge for Christians as "a reminder of their own past."[3]

These perspectives now allow us, perhaps for the first time in Western history, to begin to see Jesus as neither an orthodox Christian nor a Jew, but as a teacher influenced by the spirituality of the Middle East in general—as what I call a "native Middle Eastern" person.

No doubt, "historical" Jesus research has given us much of value. In addition to the above, it has also helped identify, at least theoretically, a core of Jesus' wisdom sayings that may be the most ancient. In some cases, however, judgments about authenticity are still based on presumptions about what early Christianity was like. As I will discuss later, barring the discovery of some definitive ancient manuscript, scholars are unlikely to arrive at any general agreement about what Jesus said and did using the methods of historical Jesus research.

This book complements historical Jesus research by presenting the interpretive methods of Middle Eastern spirituality. I recognize the value of both faith-based and scholarly approaches. Throughout the book, and in a brief afterword, I have attempted to place what is essentially a work of spiritual interpretation and inspiration within the context of current biblical studies. I am willing to leave open the question of what Jesus definitively said and did. Considering all that we know from the witnesses of the canonical Gospels, from non-canonical books like the Gospel of Thomas, and from the various hypothetical textual strands identified by scholars, there is much that Jesus could have said and done.

This book makes a simple proposition based on the following fact: *when* or *if* Jesus said anything that is attributed to him in any of these texts, he said it in Aramaic (or possibly Hebrew when quoting from scripture). For this reason, looking at Jesus' words in Aramaic reveals the spirituality of his teachings in light of the Middle Eastern tradition as a whole. Jesus may indeed have been influenced by the Hellenistic culture present in certain areas of Palestine, but the overwhelming number of people in his audience were not Greek speakers. They spoke Aramaic as their mother tongue, which since at least the third century BCE had been the common spoken language not only of Palestine but of the entire Middle East.[4] In addition, people *heard* the words of Jesus, rather than read them. In the oral tradition that followed him, people repeated and meditated upon his sayings and stories in a circular, spiritual way, not a linear, theological, or Western historical one.

THE TEXTS

We do not have any Gospel manuscripts in Palestinian Aramaic, the dialect that Jesus would have spoken. The translation I have used for my study is the bible of the Eastern Christians, called the Peshitta, which is written in Western Aramaic, often called Syriac by Western scholars. The earliest manuscript copy of the Peshitta dates to the fourth century CE. Today, Aramaic-speaking Christians of various denominations claim it as the original form of Jesus' words. To justify this claim, they point to many idioms (like "poor in spirit") that make perfect sense in Aramaic but remain obscure in Greek. Western scholars, on the other hand, are convinced that the Peshitta is a translation backward from Greek into Western Aramaic.[5]

For my purposes, this doesn't matter. I do not determine the validity of what Jesus may have said or done based on the Peshitta. I am also not attempting to recreate an original Aramaic text from it.[6] What Jesus said or did remains for each person to decide for her or himself, based on the alleged evidence, the philosophical presumptions that determine what a person recognizes as fact, and her or his own beliefs. This holds true whether the person is an agnostic academic or a fundamentalist Christian. The Peshitta is the most Semitic—the most Jewish if you will—of all of the early versions of the New Testament. At the very least, it offers us a view of Jesus' thought, language, culture, and spirituality through the eyes of a very early community of Eastern Jewish Christians. No Greek text can give us this view.

The selection of themes I have chosen for this book remain valid no matter what dialect of Aramaic Jesus may have used. Like the word "good" carrying the meaning of "ripe," my interpretations attempt to recover the Middle Eastern mind-set of Jesus and his listeners and to derive practical wisdom from it. To do this, I work with the native code present in all Semitic languages. The Aramaic version also allows me to use a style of interpretation similar to Jewish *midrash*. This style most closely approximates the way these sayings would have been heard and experienced then—with many different ears and in many different ways.

In addition to the Aramaic version of the canonical Gospels, I have also referred to sections of the Gospel of Thomas, which most scholars now believe was also originally collected and composed by Eastern Jewish Christians in Syria in the first century. The most complete copy we have of the Gospel of Thomas is in Coptic, a form of the old Egyptian language written primarily in Greek characters. Where I have quoted this text, I have combined several scholarly translations of this Coptic manuscript. I will say more about this in the first chapter.

Where I have juxtaposed an Aramaic translation with a standard English one, I have used the Authorized or King James version (KJV) for the latter. I have done so not because it is the most accurate translation of the Greek, but because it has been the most influential psychologically for most English speakers. It is the most often quoted in literature and sayings that cut across all religious boundaries. Where I have made reference to the Greek version of the Gospels, this is to the standard scholarly text edited by Nestle-Aland.

THE ORGANIZATION OF THIS BOOK

The themes explored in this book are drawn from my study of Jesus' words in Aramaic over the past seventeen years. Some of this research was the basis for my previous books, *Prayers of the Cosmos* and *Desert Wisdom*. Those books are collections of multi-leveled translations, with notes and meditations that illustrate various themes or passages. *Prayers of the Cosmos* focuses primarily on multiple readings of the Lord's Prayer and Beatitudes based on the Aramaic text. *Desert Wisdom* is broader in scope and includes many different writings from the Middle East, organized to show how the various voices commented on key life themes: What is my purpose in life? How can I know myself? What is my relationship to others? I composed both books so that a reader could browse, search through, or select from them in many different ways, according to her or his needs at the moment. With this style I sought to approximate the oral, storytelling way in which one would receive this wisdom from a Middle Eastern spiritual teacher.

The Hidden Gospel is a bit different, in that it is meant to be read from beginning to end. Each chapter presents an essay on what I consider one of the most important aspects of Jesus' Middle Eastern worldview. Most chapters juxtapose the Western and Aramaic/Hebrew senses of key words in Jesus' recorded teaching.

In each chapter I illustrate a Middle Eastern way of looking at Jesus' teaching and provide examples translated from the sayings and stories contained in the Aramaic version of the recorded Gospels. In the beginning chapters, I also reflect on the background that reveals, for me, a "hidden Gospel," the ways we can uncover it, and its implications for the relationship of humans to nature and the divine. I also gradually lay the groundwork for the interpretive methods I use, which are part of a long tradition in the Middle East.

As I reflect on each theme, I attempt to open up to the extent possible the meanings of each key word in Aramaic. Readers can then begin to make their own interpretations and translations as they meditate on these and other words of Jesus. I do not consider my interpretations the only correct ones. I intend to demonstrate a method of reflection and meditation, native to the Middle East, that will hopefully help revivify a person's faith and life. Because I consider certain material central to Jesus' teaching, in some cases, I have added new readings of passages that I translated in my previous books.

To supplement my own renderings, I have added an interpretive glossary at the end of the book. This lists key English words found in the usual translations of the Gospel texts I have considered, followed by their Aramaic counterparts as found in the Peshitta, plus alternative meanings. With this tool readers can begin to construct their own translations and interpretations using the same methods I have.

Interspersed with the commentary and renderings, I have also added examples of simple "body prayers," or meditations, inspired by the themes. These meditations use traditional Middle Eastern prayer methods such as sounded words, contemplation, breathing awareness, and body awareness. I have done this not to be "new age" in any sense, but to underline the fact that in a Middle Eastern way of sacred interpretation, translation *is* spiritual practice and is usually accompanied by prayer and meditation. In this tradition, the words of a prophet or mystic are not dead text, an object existing outside of oneself, but rather a living, breathing reality that one embodies as one hears, remembers, repeats, and meditates upon them.

I have attempted to keep the endnotes to a minimum because I intend this book to be primarily inspirational and experiential. It can easily be read through without reference to the notes. However, readers who wish to follow up the threads of this work that connect to other biblical or psychological scholarship can do so through the endnotes, which are keyed to the bibliography. The endnotes also contain formal transliterations of all the Aramaic words that I translate or interpret, for the benefit of those who wish to do their own comparative Semitic language research. In some cases, one endnote gives the transliterations for several words in a given phrase or passage, in order to cut down on the number of notes. The transliterations are keyed by number to the glossary. In the main text, I use approximate transliterations of Aramaic or Hebrew words where necessary, so that readers can use them in the body prayers or see their relationship to other key words. Finally, the endnotes also contain references to related biblical or Middle Eastern texts that can provide food for further study. In this sense, this book, like my previous ones, can be read on a number of different levels.

PERSONAL BACKGROUND

In keeping with the style of Middle Eastern interpretation, which emphasizes personal experience, it is appropriate that I should relate some of my own personal background. While part of my family comes from a Jewish background, I was raised Christian, and for the past twenty-three years I have studied both traditions as well various mystical traditions of Islam, including Sufism. I consider myself a practicing Sufi, as I believe this spiritual path enables me to receive the wisdom from all of these traditions. From an academic standpoint my background and doctorate are in both religious studies (in particular, hermeneutics, the science of interpretation) and psychology (in particular, the body-oriented psychologies of the religious traditions of the world). For ten years I taught this combination of textual interpretation and psychology at the university level. My experiential background includes the privilege of learning from many Jewish, Christian, and Sufi mystics, both hidden and known, and many Middle Eastern people throughout the world.

I believe that, like them, Jesus was a breathing, flesh-and-blood person. His Middle Eastern name was Yeshua, a form similar to the biblical name usually spelled Joshua, meaning "Ya—the Sacred Life—will save or preserve." Throughout the book, I alternate the names Jesus and Yeshua, using the latter where I emphasize his Middle Eastern background. Whatever Yeshua himself may have felt his mission to be, he inspired developments that profoundly affect the world two thousand years later.

To affirm Jesus as a native Middle Eastern person not only opens up the insights I have presented in this book, it also enables Christians to understand that the mind and message of the prophet they revere arise from the same earth as have the traditions of their Jewish and Muslim sisters and brothers. In the recognition of this fact lies the power to overcome centuries of mistrust and tragedy. How far back this tragic divide began is not the subject of this book. My purpose is to build bridges of meaning that can help connect the lovers and devotees of Jesus of all traditions, as well as all who have been inspired by his words and example.

If these efforts have some merit, it goes to my teachers. If there is benefit, let it be toward the next two thousand years, when—by the will of the One—the wisdom of a native Middle Eastern Jesus takes its rightful place in the discussions and actions that determine the future of our planet.

Chapter One

THE HIDDEN GOSPEL

SOMEWHERE IN THE JUDAEAN DESERT . . .
OR IN THE HILLS ABOVE THE DEAD SEA . . .
OR IN THE GREEN MOUNTAINS OF GALILEE . . .

A wandering Bedouin stumbles upon a cave. In the cave, he finds a crumbling urn containing an ancient manuscript with leather pages. He realizes immediately that things of this sort fetch a good price, so he takes the manuscript home and later sells it to an infamous trader on the antiquities black market. The trader begins to carefully open the manuscript, which barely holds together in his shaking hands. His fragmentary knowledge of ancient scripts, including Aramaic, allows him to read the words "Yeshua bar Alaha" within the first few lines of the text: "Jesus, Son of God."

At this point in our story, various church officials, scholars, and military intelligence officers hear of the document and begin to hunt for it. As an elaborate game of deception unfolds, the manuscript grows in reputation: it is said to contain a previously undiscovered gospel of a first-century Jewish prophet and reformer. Those in the hunt become more desperate. They begin to lie and steal to obtain the document. Those who have it, including scholars, hoard it so that no one else can see it.

With numerous variations this story has been told, as history or fiction, for the greater part of the past century. The discoveries in 1945 of the Dead Sea Scrolls as well as the ancient library found near Nag Hammadi, Egypt, have followed this general storyline. Today, there are still many unexplored caves in the areas where Jesus or his early followers could have traveled. Tomorrow may bring a find that totally revolutionizes the way we look at Jesus and early Christianity. Or perhaps, the find has already been made, and the crucial manuscript is being held privately. All of this remains the subject of enormous popular speculation.

A strong undercurrent runs throughout this story and its variations: the suspicion that Jesus did and said things that are not contained within the four canonical Gospels approved by orthodox Christianity. The Gospel of Thomas, for instance, discovered as part of the Nag Hammadi Library, shows us a Jesus who speaks like a Jewish mystic:

> *Let him who seeks, not cease seeking until he finds, and when he finds, he will be troubled, and when he has been troubled, he will marvel and he will reign over the All.* (Saying 2)

Are these words simply the fabrication of an early group of pre-Christians whom scholars usually call gnostics? To what extent do they reflect the actual words of Jesus? Most scholars date the composition of the Gospel of Thomas in the first century CE. This makes it one of the oldest gospel texts in existence. It appears to have been first collected by Jewish Christians in the region of Eastern Syria, an area not usually mentioned in the history of what became Western Christianity. And so the mysteries about Jesus' authentic words continue and lead us back further.

THREE HUNDRED YEARS OF DIVERSITY

According to the most current research, early pre-Christianity reflected tremendous diversity. While we may think of modern Christianity as divided into many branches of Protestant, Roman Catholic, and Eastern Orthodox varieties, there were many more groups in the early Jesus movement within the first two hundred years after Jesus' life. Many people held very diverse ideas about what Jesus said and did. We could call all these people Jewish Christians or Christian Jews, but as noted in the introduction, neither term identifies a single orthodox group or family of groups in the first or second centuries. According to one source, there were hundreds of different versions of Jesus' words, hundreds of "gospels," in the first three centuries after his death.[1]

As the remembered words and acts of Jesus were gradually put into writing, this diversity began to diminish. The process by which an oral transmission turns into a written one always involves selection, and the selection each group of followers makes determines its stand on important issues. In addition, those who could not read were largely left out of the decision-making process.[2] With many written gospels in existence, the diversity within early pre-Christianity continued for three hundred years, until the Roman emperor Constantine, newly converted to a variety of the faith, realized that a stable empire could not be built upon hundreds of conflicting interpretations of who Jesus was. In 325 CE he ordered a council of bishops and theologians to gather at Nicaea (in what is now Turkey) to settle once and for all who Jesus was and what he said and did. The theological portion of the debate centered on whether Jesus was human, divine, or some combination of both. There was reportedly a certain pressure on all who attended: if Constantine did not get the agreement of opinion he wanted, he might withdraw his support from Christianity altogether.[3]

Given this pressure, various compromises were made. For instance, since the sun god was very popular in Roman culture, the council declared the Roman "sun" day to be the Christian sabbath. This day of the week had no particular significance for Jesus or his early followers. Likewise, the council adopted the traditional celebration of the birth of the sun, around the time of the winter solstice, for the celebration of Jesus' birthday. The council also adopted the traditional symbol of the sun, the cross of light, to be the official emblem of Christianity. Before this time, the cross rarely figured in any Christian art or tomb decoration. Nor did any images of Jesus himself generally appear before this time because of the Jewish Christian wariness of idolatry.

On the theological side, the council composed the Nicene Creed—another compromise that a number of the council members neither fully supported nor fully understood but put their names to in order to please the emperor. The creed solved the question of whether Jesus was human or divine with obscure words, describing Jesus as "begotten, not made, being of one substance with the Father." The creed also established some version of what is called the Trinity—a belief in God as Father, Son, and Holy Spirit—as an orthodox doctrine of the Western Christian church. However, a large number, perhaps even a majority, of Christians at the time believed that God is one and indivisible, as the Jewish scriptures taught and as the name for God, *Alaha* (which means Unity), clearly states in Jesus' own tongue, Aramaic. By one account, in the years following the council at Nicaea and the two subsequent councils at Ephesus and Chalcedon, at least one million of these early "unitarian" Jewish Christians were killed because of their beliefs.[4]

Furthermore, the council at Nicaea banned all versions and variations of the Gospels except Matthew, Mark, Luke, and John. According to one contemporary but perhaps apocryphal account, the decision was made in the following way: One day the hundreds of gospels and accounts of Jesus' teachings that were available at the time were placed under a table in the meeting hall. At the end of the day, everyone left, the hall was locked, and all of the assembled bishops were asked to pray that the true gospels would miraculously appear on top of the table by the next morning. The next day, only the books of Matthew, Mark, Luke, and John were on the table. There is no report of who held the key to the room overnight. Whether this account is true or not, from that time onward, the alternative versions of Jesus' life and words were either hidden (like the Gospel of Thomas) or destroyed. We know about some of them, like the Gospel of the Hebrews, only because they are mentioned in the writings of the early church officials who opposed them.

Undoubtedly, all religions have elements of their history that would sadden the prophet upon whom the religion is based. Some of it can be explained as simple human nature: the early pre-Christians, for instance, had been persecuted for many years under the Roman Empire, and once they saw the opportunity to gain imperial sponsorship, the temptation was irresistible.[5] And yet, because we know that so many accounts were destroyed in the process, and because the religion that claims Jesus' name has been so influential in Western culture, the search for the definitive version of his words continues.

MORE HIDDEN GOSPELS

In the past one hundred years, scholars have searched for a "hidden Gospel" in a different way as well. By examining various textual strands in the books of Matthew, Mark, and Luke, they have posited hypothetical sources that the writers of these books used. The most well known, called "Q" (for the German word *Quelle*, or source) consists essentially of the duplicate portions of Matthew and Luke that do not also appear in Mark. The hypothesis runs as follows: Most scholars now consider Mark to be the earliest written Gospel of which we have a copy. If the authors of Matthew and Luke were not aware of each other's work, then the portions of these two books that do not use Mark as a source and that overlap must have used another source: Q.

Like the Gospel of Thomas, Q is proposed to be a collection of sayings, aphorisms, and parables, with very few actual events recorded in it. Many scholars now consider these early textual strands to be the products of various evolving Jesus movement communities. It is important, however, to recognize that this entire theoretical structure is based upon the presumptions mentioned above. While these scholars see their work as historical, it is still theory, and all of the theorists do not even agree.[6]

But there is yet another story of a "hidden Gospel," this one rarely told. At the time of the council of Nicaea, the eastern areas of what are now Turkey, Syria, and Iraq were controlled by the Persian Empire. In this region, a group of early Christians had established themselves securely by the time of the destruction of Jerusalem by the Romans in 70 CE. The early Jewish Christians in Persian lands were largely of Semitic extract, and all were Aramaic-speaking. Since the Persians were enemies of the Romans, and since the Romans persecuted the Christians, the Persians decided to let these Christians practice their religion in peace (another instance of the old axiom: the enemy of my enemy must be my friend). These early Christians built schools, libraries, and places of worship in the Persian Empire, with Persian support, throughout the time that the Romans persecuted the Christians in European and Mediterranean areas.

For the first four centuries of the Christian era, Aramaic-speaking Christians in these lands had copies of early scriptures that they could study and contemplate in their homes openly and without fear of reprisal.[7] In the earliest days, these included the Gospel of Thomas, which was most likely compiled in what is now Syria, and which reflects a view of Jesus as a wisdom figure rather than a savior.

The version of the scriptures these Jewish Christians used originated around Edessa in what is now eastern Turkey and came to be known as the Peshitta—meaning simple, straight, and true. The Peshitta included the basic Gospels—Matthew, Mark, Luke, and John—but in a form of Aramaic close to the dialect that Jesus himself would have used.[8]

Since they spoke and worshipped in the same language that Yeshua spoke, these Aramaic Christians felt (and their descendants still feel) that the Peshitta is a version of the original Aramaic words of Jesus, and that they stayed very close in spirit to his original message. While some Aramaic-speaking Jewish Christian groups went along with the council of Nicaea, most soon broke contact with the rest of both Roman and Eastern Orthodox Christianity over the increasingly complex creeds and the forceful attempts to impose a single theology on all Christians. Little was heard from or reported about them in Europe for the next fifteen hundred years, while Christianity in the West underwent its own political and theological evolution.

As modern Assyrian Christian writer Abraham Rihbany commented:

> [T]he Syrian Christians of Semitic stock have had very little to do with the development of the "creeds of Christendom." Theological organization has been as foreign to the minds of the Eastern Christians as political organization. They have always been worshippers rather than theologians, believers rather than systematic thinkers. . . . The Christian Church had its simple origin with a group of Jewish followers of Jesus Christ in Palestine. . . . The creed of the theologians consists of many "articles"; the creed of Christ only two: "Love the Lord thy God with all thy heart, and thy neighbor as thyself."[9]

Another Aramaic Christian scholar, George Lamsa, pointed out the irony that most Christians in Europe were not allowed to read the scriptures until well after the advent of the printing press in the Middle Ages; until that time only priests were allowed to see the scriptures. Even the possession of a translation of the Gospels in a vernacular language like English was a crime punishable by death. On the other hand, a thousand years earlier, Aramaic-speaking Christians had copies of the Gospels in Aramaic in their homes and for their open use.

THE MIND OF MIDDLE EASTERN SPIRITUALITY

As both Lamsa and Rihbany note, the mind of a Semitic language speaker inherently divides and makes sense of reality differently than that of a Greek or Latin speaker. As people of the West, we have been raised with many Greek and European language concepts. We have been taught that they constitute the essence of civilization and science, and so we take them for granted. However, there are other equally valid ways to view the world.

For instance, as we shall explore later, both Aramaic and Hebrew have only one preposition that must describe both the relationship "within" (as in "within my interior, emotional life") and "among" (as in "among my exterior social community"). When "within" and "among" are the same word, then the way in which I treat the different voices within me—my interior "selves"—is always connected to the way I treat my friends, neighbors, and enemies—my exterior "selves." In addition, the Greek division of human life into "mind," "body," "emotions," "psyche," and "spirit" underlies the modern Western view. The Semitic languages do not divide reality in this way. They provide multiple words for the subconscious self, all tied to the communal self. They imply a continuum between what we call spirit and body, not a division.

We may think of this as mysticism, but again the distinction between the mystical and the prophetic is also the result of later speculation and thought grounded in the Greek language. Academics usually speak of mysticism as an esoteric teaching imparted to only a few, or pursued in solitude by ascetics. They define prophecy as an exoteric, socially critical teaching that seeks to change outer affairs. This division does not exist in Hebrew, Aramaic, or Arabic. Likewise, the Western view of what constitutes "history" is prejudiced by a language that separates inner from outer. The Western view divides cosmology, that is, the way we view our place in the universe, from psychology, the way we view our inner life. It considers neither to be the stuff of historical or scientific facts. The Semitic language view differs entirely from the Western, reflecting the notion that there is a single community that includes everything from planets to the voices of the subconscious.

Jesus was born an Aramaic speaker, as were the vast majority of his listeners. An Aramaic version of Jesus' reported words allows us at the very least to witness the view that a very early group of Jewish Christians held of what Jesus taught. But more than that, it allows us to participate in the richness of the Aramaic mind-set, with all of the ambiguities and paradoxes present in its spirituality, that is, in its experience of the sacred.

DECODING THE HIDDEN GOSPEL

If we consider Jesus' words in Aramaic, we can then participate in an important Semitic language tradition: translation and interpretation as personal spiritual practices, rather than as academic pursuits. The practices themselves have many layers and nuances. The next several chapters will gradually increase our acquaintance with them.

To begin with, a single word in Aramaic or Hebrew can often mean several seemingly different things. For instance, the Aramaic word *shema* (as well as its Semitic root ShM, or *shem*) can mean light, sound, name, or atmosphere. If we consider the admonition of Jesus to pray "with or in my *shem*" (usually translated "in my name"), which meaning is intended? According to Middle Eastern tradition, in the words of sacred scripture or the words of a prophet all possible meanings may be present. One needs then to look at a given statement several different ways. In addition, Aramaic and Hebrew lend themselves to rich and poetic wordplay, like inner rhyming of vowels, repetition of consonant sounds, and parallel phrasing. These devices further increase the possible translations and interpretations of a given statement.

When a root word like *shem* becomes modified, its meanings may expand further. For instance, the first line of the prayer usually called the Lord's Prayer or "Our Father" contains the word *shem-aya*, usually translated "heaven." The ending added to *shem* implies that its effect extends without limit. In order to hear more of the possibilities of this first line, one needs to render the phrase from the Aramaic Gospels, *Abwoon d'bashmaya*, several different ways—something like this:

> *O Thou, the One from whom*
> *breath enters being in*
> *all radiant forms.*
>
> *O Parent of the universe, from your*
> *deep interior comes the next wave*
> *of shining life.*
>
> *O fruitful, nurturing Life-giver!*
> *Your sound rings everywhere*
> *throughout the cosmos.*
>
> *Father-Mother who births Unity,*
> *You vibrate life into form*
> *in each new instant.*[10]

The King James version gives us "Our Father which art in heaven." Three hundred years later, the New Jerusalem Bible improved this only by shortening it slightly to "Our Father in heaven." In both, the additional nuances and suggestions of the Aramaic, which would have been heard by the Semitic listener, are missing. It's not that these English translations are wrong; they are simply very limited. They can't hold the spiritual possibilities of the original Aramaic—and there are many others, even for this one line of the prayer. Metaphorically, they are like fruit juice that has been strained through a very fine filter and heated, leaving all of the valuable vitamins, minerals, trace elements, and pulp behind.[11]

Each stanza of my poetic translation above is itself incomplete, yet points toward a unity that is only expressed in the Aramaic words themselves: *Abwoon d'bashmaya.* Likewise, when read aloud, one line may be heard more clearly than another by a particular person, depending upon her or his life experience. According to the Middle Eastern tradition of spiritual interpretation, this would be the translation of the moment for that person.

In this tradition of translation and interpretation, the words of a prophet or mystic—stories, prayers, and visionary statements—challenge listeners to understand them according to their own life experience. These traditions propose that we can only fix the meaning of a sacred text at a particular time and place in relation to our own life experience. This type of translation-interpretation not only bridges languages, but also connects that which can be said in language and that which remains a wordless experience. It is a "translation" between our outer and inner lives, as well as between our lives as individuals and as members of a community. As we look at the major themes in Yeshua's teaching, we need to remember that the search we are engaged in is for our own souls, rather than for some so-called objective notion of who Jesus was. In a Middle Eastern sense, this book can be heard as a series of stories and lessons toward this end.

TOOLS FOR THE SEARCH

In this book I bring together tools that open up the meaning of Jesus' words and place these words firmly in the context of his native language, ecology, culture, and spirituality. To recap, these tools are:

- The Aramaic language, as well as its cultural background
- The shared worldview, psychology, and cosmology of related Semitic languages and cultures, including Hebrew and Arabic
- The tradition of mystical translation and interpretation associ-

ated with these languages

- The spiritual practices that arise from this worldview and tradition of interpretation
- Various early Christian reports of Jesus' words, including the four canonical Gospels (in the Aramaic version) and the Gospel of Thomas (in the Coptic and fragmentary Greek versions)

Bringing together all these tools, we possess a powerful means for seeing Jesus through a native Middle Eastern lens. Figuratively, we put on a pair of eyeglasses that allow us to perceive reality in depth rather than in two dimensions. Hopefully, as we progress chapter by chapter through this book, the depth of field will fill in and increase for the viewer, so that the real Gospel hidden behind the usual translations reveals itself.

This process is made difficult because so much has been written and said about Jesus in the past two thousand years. To use another image, we are attempting to restore the natural wildflowers, plants, and trees to a particular area after it has been over-cultivated or over-grazed.

A current and popular academic view says that all we can really do is determine a picture of the early Christian communities that created the texts we have; all else is supposition, and we can find no "real" Jesus behind any of the texts. We can say with safety that truth is relative. But life is not safe. It constantly asks us to make decisions based on our own, often intuitive, sense of what feels right in a given situation. We carry this intuitive sense of wisdom with us at all times. It can be enlarged and enriched with practice and contemplation. My purpose here is reveal a hidden resource to do this: the wisdom of Jesus.

In relation to early Christian communities, I am making one major assumption: these groups did not simply fabricate anything they wanted Jesus to say. No doubt additions were made to various texts. But a natural process of transmission from an oral tradition to a written one involves remembrance and selection. Various groups selected the parables and sayings they remembered from oral tradition and felt were important. They left out other sayings and wove their own interpretations around them, as a storyteller would do today. Even in the so-called factual world of Western journalism, we find that reporters select the facts they consider important, which are often rewritten by editors, and sometimes publishers, who never witnessed the events at all.

When we look primarily at the sayings and stories of Jesus, as the Gospel of Thomas and the early Q strands of Matthew and Luke do, rather than at the later, theological claims about his person and status, we come face-to-face with a native mystic of the Middle East. Even the Gospel of John (considered a more theologized work by many scholars) reveals many elements of a Jewish mystical background.[12] While there has been much speculation that Jesus may have received the essence of his teaching elsewhere, in India or Greece for example, I don't find anything in his prophetic or mystical teaching that implies a source outside the broader traditions of the Middle East. These include not only various Jewish traditions, but also those of Egyptian wisdom and other indigenous folk traditions active at the time.

WHY UNDERTAKE THE HUNT?

Does any of this really make a difference to anything more than our personal spiritual experience, as important as this may be? I believe that it makes an enormous difference in the way we view both each other and our place in the natural world.

Yeshua lived in a world where the sacred and the natural were part of each other, not separated by a wide gulf. As we shall see, the division between heaven and earth, which we take for granted, is the result of an inadequate translation and interpretation of a very profound Jewish creation story.

When Western Christianity made the choices it did fifteen hundred or so years ago, it not only created theological creeds that limited the support for individual spiritual experience, but it also weakened the links between humanity, nature, and the divine. The tendency to limit diversity in spiritual experience carried over to a tendency to limit and control the natural world, for the purposes of advancing what we call civilization. Now many of us have begun to question just what sort of civilization this is that has brought us to the brink of ecological disaster.

From a Middle Eastern point of view, if the divine is truly Unity, then the particular evolution of Western Christianity must have been for a particular purpose. This includes the difficulties it has had contacting its original earth-based, Middle Eastern roots and the tragic results of these difficulties. Until now, the "hidden Gospel" has lain buried deep within the Western psyche, perhaps awaiting just this moment to be discovered. As we unearth this real treasure, I believe we will discover the missing link to our collective Western soul and find the solutions to the problems that confront us in the world today.

Part One

New Adam: Experiencing Original Creation

Chapter Two

ΛLΛHΛ: IOOPROVISΛTIONS IN THE KEY OF UNITY

Ripe are the consistent in heart; they shall see Sacred Unity everywhere.

> —a reading of Matthew 5:8 from the Aramaic
> (KJV: "Blessed are the pure in heart:
> for they shall see God.")

Remain within yourselves—live in a place of rooted confidence in Sacred Unity.

> —a reading of Mark 11:22 from the Aramaic
> (KJV: "Have faith in God.")

IN ARAMAIC, THE NAME *ALAHA*[1] REFERS TO THE DIVINE, AND WHEREVER YOU READ THE WORD "GOD" IN A QUOTE FROM YESHUA, YOU CAN INSERT THIS WORD. IT MEANS VARIOUSLY: SACRED UNITY, ONE-ness, the All, the Ultimate Power/Potential, the One with no opposite. It is related to the name of God in Hebrew, *Elohim*, which is based on the same root word: EL or AL.[2] This root could be translated literally as the sacred "The," since it is also used as the definite article in Hebrew, Aramaic, and Arabic.

If we think deeply into this, we find it suggests that every definite "article"—every unique being—should remind us of the one Unity. If only one Being exists, then every other being must have a share in it. Individuality is only relative in this view of God.

27

By contrast, the English word "God" is based on a Germanic root meaning good. No doubt, we can see goodness as one aspect of the divine, but it is not the same as unity. Goodness does not, by definition, include everything, nor does it include whatever we choose to define as evil. Later, we will take a look at the additional meanings that the Aramaic language gives to the words for good and evil.

Today, Arabic-speaking Christians in the Middle East still use a form of this word for Unity—*Allah*—to refer to the divine. We find that it is not a word used exclusively by Muslims, but simply refers to the primary concept of the divine in the Middle East for the past two to four thousand years. Even before the Jewish scriptures were composed, some people in the Middle East used a form of this word—*Allat* or *Elat*—to refer to Sacred Unity idealized as the Middle Eastern Great Goddess.

Variations on the theme of Unity run throughout the Middle Eastern traditions. The ancient Hebrew form—*Elohim*—has a plural ending, which can be interpreted many ways—"the One that is also Many" or "Unity in Diversity." The Great Goddess form *Elat* emphasizes "the One that is Embodied, Here and Now." By comparison, both the Aramaic form *Alaha* and the Arabic *Allah* emphasize Unity without qualification or limit.

To contemplate or to chant one of these names is a profound spiritual practice in a number of Middle Eastern traditions today. In addition, one Jewish mystical practice is a meditation on the "nameless Name," the word that cannot be spoken. This practice emphasizes that whatever concepts we may hold of the divine, the mystery of Sacred Unity is still beyond them.

We will encounter various Middle Eastern spiritual practices in our investigation of the hidden Gospel. Because these practices are about experiential learning, I have inserted body prayers based on them at intervals in this book. I suggest that you take a few moments for each meditation before reading further in order to cultivate your own spiritual experience of the themes we explore.

THE PRESENCE OF UNITY

The practice of the presence of Unity can take us directly into the atmosphere of the Aramaic Jesus.

Settle yourself for a few moments, and breathe easily and gently. Place one hand very lightly over the heart and experience the sensation of your breathing there, in the middle of what Jesus would have called the leba³—the center of courage and feeling. As you breathe in, feel the sound "A-la-ha," and as you breathe out, feel the same sound. Let the rhythm of the sound and the rhythm of your own breath come into a harmony of feeling. After some minutes, release the sound of the word and simply practice the presence of Unity: all inner voices and concerns are acknowledged and included; all outer voices and concerns are acknowledged and included—without judgment. During another session, you might begin by chanting the name Alaha on one note a few times, then breathe the word, and finally release it, allowing the feeling to lead you into the silence.

CONCEPTS OF GOD

Our usual Western concepts of God and the sacred are only a partial view of Sacred Unity in the Middle Eastern sense. It is difficult to overemphasize this point. Most of us have been raised from childhood to think of God as a being infinitely distant from humanity or nature, and of the sacred as something separate from the profane. We have been taught that religion operates by different rules than politics, science, psychology, art, or culture. Yeshua's teaching and reported dealings with his followers show that he did not live from this type of separation thinking.

Indeed, it should have been difficult for anyone at his time to entirely divorce Alaha from the way that one related to one's community, to nature, or to the political forces of the time.

In the Gospel of Thomas, various sayings of Yeshua point to Alaha as Sacred Unity:[4]

> *Look for the Living One while you are alive, so that you will not die and then seek to see him and be unable to see.* (Saying 59)

> *On the day when you were One, you became two; but when you have become two, what will you do?* (Saying 11:4)

The Jesus of the Gospel of Thomas also repeatedly uses phrases like "and they shall stand as a single one"—sometimes translated as "solitary one." Certainly these expressions point to a wandering, preaching lifestyle, exemplified by Jesus himself. I believe they also point to the Middle Eastern concept of the divine as Unity, without opposites. This concept also appears in the following saying:

> *When you make the two One, and when you make the inner as the outer and the outer as the inner, and the above as the below . . . then you will enter the kingdom.* (Saying 22:4,7)

We may think that this ideal of the sacred is more profound than Western ideas of God as a separate, superhuman figure. Yet Oneness can also be twisted into exclusivity, as in "I am the only one who has the truth." In Yeshua's eyes, those in charge of the worship at the Jerusalem Temple manipulated their position to exclude or take advantage of those who were lesser in class, wealth, or position. Yeshua repeatedly criticized those who have the teachings of Oneness yet do not act on them and do not allow others access to them either.[5]

Some people who came to Yeshua thought that spiritual and religious change required political revolution. Many wanted Yeshua to take a political position and lead an armed rebellion. Unity could be taken to mean: "Political unity first—overthrow the Romans, and we'll worry about the rest later." In fact, before, during, and after the time of Yeshua, a number of alternate messiahs (anointed ones), kings, and prophets roused crowds of people to armed rebellion.[6]

However, Yeshua's reported sayings emphasize that if *Alaha* really meant Unity, a change of heart was necessary before a change of government. Otherwise the oppression that his listeners experienced would only reappear in a new form. In the words of his parable, the "unripe spirits" would reenter the house swept clean, in more profusion than before.[7] The faces would change but the poor would still suffer. But if there were a communal change of heart, a violent solution would not be necessary, or even thinkable. There would really be a new reign of empowerment in which those who suffered now could rejoice.

We may think this very idealistic, but when one stands by the power of Alaha, as Yeshua and the prophets of the ancient Jewish tradition did, even seeming miracles are possible. Any being can bring through the power of Unity, since ultimately separation does not exist.

The Power of Miracles

The idea of Sacred Unity has everything to do with the stories of Jesus' miracles. The Western idea of a "super-natural" event takes for granted that nature is neither conscious nor sacred. In the Middle Eastern view, however, events are always embedded in Sacred Unity, even when we don't understand their purpose.

Let us look, for example, at the story of Jesus healing the deaf and dumb man in Mark 7:32-37. Here we find that all versions of the Gospels, including those from the Greek, state that he uses a healing word of power in Aramaic—"Eth-phatah"—which is rendered "be opened."[8] This word has resonances at least as far back as the old Egyptian god-name,

Ptah, who was considered the opener or the open mouth that created the world. This aspect of the Egyptian mysteries emphasized a process of opening to the divine, creating space, and then shaping it into words and actions for creation and for healing. Some part of this tradition may have survived into Jesus' time. Likewise, the biblical Hebrew uses another form of the word in the same sense—as a creative opening to the sacred, as well as an expression of redemption—as in Psalm 118:19: "Open to me the gates of righteousness: I will go into them, and I will praise the Lord."

If we set the scene for this healing, using the Aramaic version as the source, we find several details that take us to the heart of Yeshua's vision of the healing power of Alaha:

First, Yeshua took the man aside, so the crowd could not see, and placed his fingers gently into the man's ears. This spiritual practice still exists in several traditions to this day, including that of the Middle Eastern Sufis. The effect is to turn the sensation of the sense around, from outer to inner. One listens toward the inside rather than the outside and follows the body awareness of hearing back to its source. It is not really the ears that hear, but a capacity inside that interprets the vibrations as sound. Modern science identifies this capacity with part of the nervous system or brain, yet this does not explain how we organize the flood of vibrations we receive. In the ancient Middle East, this "Sacred Sense," which interprets all individual senses, was called *Hokhmah* (or *Sophia* in Greek, about whom more later). If the sacred is ultimately Unity, there must be one Sense to which all senses and sensations return.

Next, as they breathed together, Yeshua drew closer, spat on the ground, and touched the man's tongue. By doing so, he united his sensing self with the other. Various healing traditions in the Middle East still use this type of body-to-body contact. The resonance of the healer's breathing brings the patient into the same rhythm. The aliveness of the healer's touch and awareness brings those of the patient back into wholeness.

Then, as Yeshua focused on the One Source of all sensation and knowing, he raised his glance and awareness upward. He breathed one long and powerful breath with *shemaya*[9]—the universe of vibration. In most translations of Mark 7:34, it is assumed that Jesus only "looked up to heaven." But the phrase in Aramaic, *har bashmaya*, could as easily mean that he contemplated or considered heaven, which in Aramaic and Hebrew refers to the universe of vibration, sound, and light.

Finally, releasing his hands from the man's ears, Yeshua said forcefully, "Ethphatah!" This can mean not only:

Be opened to the healing power of Sacred Unity

but also

Expand! Give up your small identity as a person without sound

Clear the way! Receive the healing power that is all around you

Allow yourself to be flooded by the waves of sacred space,
which give and receive all sound, hearing, and speech

Was Jesus a psychologist? Did he merely teach positive thinking or "mind over matter"? These questions, again, come from our Western materialistic mind-set, which considers mind less real than and separate from matter. Like teachers in other spiritual traditions closer to the earth, Jesus' words and actions in Aramaic show that he considered sound, word, thought, and action part of one sacred reality.

The Gospels report Yeshua saying many times that the major factor in the success of healing was a person's faith. In Aramaic, the word for faith is *haimanuta*[10]—which can also mean one's confidence, firmness, or integrity of being in Sacred Unity. From its Semitic roots, I and MN, this word indicates a connection of the sacred life force (I) through its many outer forms (MN) in a way that is rooted, renewing, and healing.

A good example is the story of the healing of the centurion's servant, found in the Q strand of both Matthew and Luke.[11] The centurion tells Yeshua that he is not worthy to have him in his house, and that all Yeshua really needs to do is command the healing to take place. "For I am a man under authority, having soldiers under me: and I say to this man, Go, and he goeth; and to another, Come, and he cometh; and to my servant, Do this, and he doeth it."

Yeshua comments, "Not even in Israel have I found faith—life-giving confidence—like this." He then says to the centurion, "As your life-giving confidence is, so things will be for you." Because Yeshua did not even meet the servant or even enter the same room with him, it was literally the centurion's own *haimanuta*—his magnetic and healing confidence—that actually did the healing when he returned home.

This word for faith is the one that I translated in an expanded way in the passage from Mark that appears at the beginning of this chapter. Here the word also implies a sense of certainty or rootedness, a "staying within" that allows one to be unshaken by phenomena outside oneself. This quality results from a practice of concentration on Unity, which allows one to heal as well as to undertake mystical contemplations, such as those found in the Jewish traditions of Jesus' time.

THE POWER OF THE WORD

We return now to unravel a bit more of the Middle Eastern tradition of translation and interpretation as spiritual practice. As in physical healing, the power of the sacred word becomes magnified in a universe suffused with Alaha, Sacred Unity. Each word is not only a mental symbol but also, like every other created being, a possible doorway into a vision of Sacred Unity. The whole concept of the sacred as Unity—

beyond names, forms, ideas, symbols, and concepts—empowers the idea that one must continually renew the meaning of sacred words and find one's own way to Unity through them.

In the Jewish mystical tradition of Kabbalah, the spiritual practice of interpretation called *midrash* begins with a study of the Hebrew letters themselves, which symbolize cosmic or universal patterns of energy. In some parts of the tradition, sacred words and letters are considered living beings, like angels.[12] Kabbalistic texts also maintain that every letter, word, phrase, and sentence of the scripture exists simultaneously on several levels of meaning. For the most part, this interpretative tradition has survived in the mystical stream of Judaism as a spiritual practice passed down orally from teacher to student.[13]

Mystical Islam maintains a similar approach to the translation and interpretation of the ninety-nine "Beautiful Names" of Allah as well as the Arabic letters and words of the Quran itself.[14] The Ismaili and Sufi mystics have preserved the most profound and complex mystical interpretive methods, called *tawil*. Like Kabbalistic *midrash*, *tawil* uses the sacred text or word as a symbol through which to contact a greater cosmic reality. Nature itself is considered a holy book, the "Quran of creation," which inspires the ideas and archetypes of all human writings.[15]

Both the Jewish and Islamic traditions of mystical interpretation point to the importance of individual letters and letter-combinations. The Semitic languages—Babylonian, Ugaritic, Aramaic, Hebrew, and Arabic (among others)—depend upon a root-and-pattern system that makes sense of such a method. Individual letters carry a force and direction that stems from the divine life. These letters then combine with others to form what are called roots, which represent new beings and families of beings. This mystical system of word roots is very much like the musical system of Indian ragas, in which families of scales interlink and "intermarry" to produce other scales. Like this improvised music, the process of learning multi-leveled translation in the Semitic languages depends as much on feeling as on technique, as much on attunement and spiritual experience as on grammatical scholarship.

HUMANITY: HEARING THE HARMONY OF UNITY

If the divine is Unity, then what is the purpose of humanity? According to one interpretation of the Jewish creation story in the Torah, the human being is part of a sacred experiment conducted by Divine Unity. This experiment centers on the following question: is it possible for one being, one particle in the vast wave of diversity, to hold within itself the consciousness of the totality?

The old Hebrew word for human being in Genesis—*adam*—refers to a non-gendered being made up of *dam*—juice, wine, sap, or essence—which has assimilated or expressed *a*—the letter *aleph*, which points to Sacred Unity. The word for wine or juice also symbolizes individual consciousness, which much of Middle Eastern sacred literature sees as distilled or fermented from Sacred Unity. According to this view of Genesis, we as human beings have been given the challenge to hold within ourselves the consciousness of all older life forms, as well as the entire universe, manifest and unmanifest.

Similarly, when Genesis talks about human beings as created in the "image" of the divine, the Hebrew text uses the word *betzallem*,[16] which can also mean a projection of Unity, a veil over the sacred that reveals its general outline, or a shadow of the totality of the Being that is both One and Many (Elohim). By this interpretation, we as humans have much to live up to.

One early Jewish mystical practice used before and at the time of Yeshua involved remembering and reexperiencing the creation story in one's own being.[17] The original archetype of *adam*, the perfection of humanity, became a focus for meditation. One reading of the first chapter of the book of John shows us that, in at least some branches of early Christianity, Yeshua was considered the embodiment of the original "word" or perfect human archetype that was present "in the beginning."

The Peshitta version of John 1:1 uses the Aramaic form for "in the beginning" (*b'rishit*)[18] that corresponds to the Hebrew word in Genesis 1:1 (*b'reshith*). To an Aramaic-speaking Jewish Christian this would immediately signal a correspondence with the creation story. The Aramaic version uses *melta*[19] for "word," which can also mean a command, a sentence, or something fully formed. If we remember that in Genesis, Elohim "speaks" creation into existence (like Ptah in the Egyptian tradition), then we have another resonance to the Hebrew creation story. When John 1:5 refers to the light shining in the darkness, again Aramaic forms are used similar to those in the Hebrew of Genesis 1:2-4 where "darkness was upon the face of the deep" and then light burst forth.

One could experience this process—returning to the primeval beginning, entering the darkness and bringing light—not simply as a mythic story, but also in one's own awareness. This contemplative practice lies at the heart of one of the most interpreted passages in the Gospels: Yeshua's interview with Nicodemus, reported in John 3:3-8, in which Yeshua says (KJV): "Verily, verily, I say unto thee, Except a man be born again, he cannot see the kingdom of God. . . . Except a man be born of water and of the spirit, he cannot enter into the kingdom of God."

For "born again," the Aramaic version uses the words *min d'rish*—be born from the beginning—which again uses the same form for archetypal "beginning" as in Genesis 1:1. The word for "water" uses the same form as that in the Hebrew of Genesis 1:2, which also means the flowing, chaotic darkness. The Aramaic word for "spirit" can also mean breath, and parallels the Hebrew of Genesis 1:2, when the "Spirit of God moved upon the face of the waters." These clues show that Jesus advocated that Nicodemus recreate the creation story within himself by returning to the primordial darkness from which the light first arose, using his own spirit-breath as a vehicle.[20]

The Gospel of Thomas quotes Yeshua advocating a similar spiritual practice in the following dialogue with his students:

> *The disciples said to Jesus: Tell us how our end will be. Jesus said: Have you then discovered the beginning so that you inquire about the end? For where the beginning is, there shall the end be also. Blessed is he who shall stand at the beginning, and he shall know the end, and he shall not taste death.* (Saying 18)

We might well ask with Nicodemus: how do we do that? One way, according to Yeshua, is to use the awareness of the breath to return in imagination to the beginning of existence. As we prepare to look more closely at Holy Breath in the next chapter, this might be good time to remember our own breath.

BREATHING WITH THE FIRST BEGINNING

Return to a relaxed yet alert position, and breathe easily and naturally. Again feel the heart as the center of awareness. As you breathe, feel again the sound A-la-ha inside and bring the light of awareness into your inner being. What voices are there waiting to be heard, what feelings that you have been forcing away? Allow the breath to go deeper into the body, at least into the belly, and as you do so, remember or imagine a time when you as the individual you are now did not exist. Remember a time when humanity itself did not exist, but was simply a potential in the great experiment of being begun by Alaha.

Hold yourself just at that point of imagination. How does it feel to be one creature among many, not the dominant force, but simply the potential for complete compassion—for feeling community with every other being? Breathe with as much compassion as you can feel at this moment for the beings that preceded you onto this planet. Also breathe with as much compassion as you can feel for all of the unresolved, chaotic, and wild aspects within yourself. Allow Alaha to include all of them in its heart.

Chapter Three

BREATH: THE SPIRIT OF LIFE[1]

God is breath.
All that breathes resides in the Only Being.
From my breath
to the air we share
to the wind that blows around the planet:
Sacred Unity inspires all.

> —alternate readings of John 4:24 from the Aramaic
> (KJV: "God is a spirit.")

Ripe are those who reside in breath;
to them belongs the reign of unity.
Blessed are those who realize that breath is
their first and last possession;
theirs is the "I Can" of the cosmos.

> —alternate readings of Matthew 5:3 from the Aramaic
> (KJV: "Blessed are the poor in spirit: for theirs
> is the kingdom of heaven.")

IN THE FOUR CANONICAL GOSPELS JESUS REFERS TO "SPIRIT" MORE THAN ONE HUNDRED TIMES. HE USES THE WORD IN EXPRESSIONS LIKE THOSE ABOVE AS WELL AS IN THE STATEMENT THAT TO SPEAK against the Holy Spirit is an unforgivable sin (KJV): "whosoever speaketh against the Holy Ghost, it shall not be forgiven him, neither in this world, neither in the world to come" (Matthew 12:32).

In both Hebrew and Aramaic, the same word—*ruha*[2] in Aramaic, *ruach* in Hebrew—must stand for several English words: spirit, wind, air, and breath. Translations that arise out of European Christianity assume that only one of these possibilities is appropriate for each passage. However, as we have seen, when we meditate on the words of a prophet or mystic in the Middle Eastern way, we must consider all possibilities simultaneously. So "Holy Spirit" must also be "Holy Breath."

This transcends word play and requires us to shift our consciousness. The separations between spirit and body, between humanity and nature, which we often take for granted in the English language, begin to fall away.

Many Western scientists admire the prophetic figure of Jesus and his reported sayings. Yet they presume that the actual wisdom and mysticism of the prophet is buried under centuries of acculturation as well as the editing of the Christian scriptures themselves. Many scientists feel that when some Christian churches rule out scientific theories like evolution and relativity in the name of Jesus, they set up an impassable barrier between science and religion. Attempts to create windows in this barrier have been pursued by both theologians and scientists.[3]

The differences may, however, have less to do with science and religion than with two different ways to view the relationship between God, humanity, and nature—the Middle Eastern and the Western. As the Western Christian church began to emphasize faith in Jesus as the definition of salvation, it excluded nature from this definition. Nature and wilderness became defined as arenas of conflict rather than contemplation. This led to the desire—almost the imperative—to conquer and control nature. In the Eastern Church, however, nature remained a support for the spiritual life and a participant in "salvation."[4]

I believe that Western culture subconsciously carries an understanding of spirit and the spiritual that is an over-materialization of Jesus' very profound and symbolic worldview. He shared this view with the Jewish prophets before him, and used it in unique sayings and stories to evoke a radical change of heart in his listeners. Many of his sayings on breath and breathing reveal a "native" wisdom that has been rediscovered only in this century by various body researchers.

SPIRIT AND TRUTH ARE BREATH AND HARMONY

Let's look at the full statement from John 4:24, rendered in part at the opening of this chapter, which is usually translated (KJV): "God is a Spirit: and they that worship him must worship him in spirit and in truth."

We have already seen how the first half of the statement differs in the Aramaic version: From the perspective of Sacred Unity, my breath is connected to the air we all breathe. It participates in the wind and in the atmosphere that surrounds the whole planet. This atmosphere then connects to the ineffable spirit-breath that pervades the seen and unseen worlds.

The Aramaic word for "worship"[5] in this passage can also mean to bow oneself or surrender. The word *sherara*,[6] translated as "truth," has several meanings in Aramaic and Hebrew: that which liberates and opens possibilities, that which is strong and vigorous, and that which acts in keeping with universal harmony. It is the sense of a right direction at a particular time that enlivens one's personal purpose and at the same time harmonizes with all. Drawing on these additional meanings, the second half of John 4:24 can also read:

Those who surrender to Unity,
bowing to it in utmost adoration,
must do so
in breath and harmony,
like the sense of right direction
that drives the universal winds.

In a very expansive way, this statement unites us with all other breathing beings in a melody of unity. In a very practical, here-and-now way, it connects us to the most diverse voices of our inner and outer worlds.

BREATH ENTERING BODY

The idea of breath coming into a body, progressively and with various effects, goes back to the Jewish scriptures in Genesis, and perhaps to the formation of the Hebrew language itself.[7] According to one interpretation of Jewish mysticism, Hebrew's four different "h" sounds, which are four different letters, represent the degrees of interpenetration of matter and breath, and its consequences:

- The letter *hey*, a very refined sound, like the *h* in the English "hear," refers to the breath that is free and unencumbered, not yet attracted by an individual body.
- The letter *heth*, like the *ch* in Scottish *loch* (no English equivalent), refers to the breath as it begins to enter a body and enliven it.
- The letter *kaph*, like *ch* in the German *ich* or "Bach," an even rougher sound than "heth," refers to the breath as it is fully embodied.
- The letter *'eh* has no precise English equivalent, but is guttural like an emphasized *e* in "they," though without the *y* sound. It represents the breath that has become overly involved in a body and trapped there. It cannot feel its connection to other expressions of breath.

In the final condition, one falls out of contact not only with the sacred, but also with other living beings. This sound, for instance, is the central root of the word for enemy in Aramaic,[8] which could also be translated "one who falls out of rhythm" in relation to someone or something else. To breathe with an exclusive focus on one's small self—the individual "I" disconnected from the sacred "I," the only being—is the definition of egotism.

"Sin against the Holy Spirit"

The notion of an egocentric breath also makes sense of the saying about the "unforgivable sin" in Matthew 12:31,[9] where Jesus says (KJV):

> *Wherefore I say unto you, All manner of sin and blasphemy shall be forgiven unto men: but the blasphemy against the Holy Ghost shall not be forgiven unto men.*

The Aramaic word translated as "sin"[10] could also mean that which misses the mark or falls into error, as well as a failure or mistake. Its root points figuratively both to frustrated hopes and to threads that have become tangled. The same root can also mean to dig out a well or furrow, or to sew, patch, or mend something. So the seeds of restoration are, so to speak, implied in what has been broken.

The Aramaic word for "blasphemy" can also mean a reviling, or more literally from the word's roots, a cutting off, incision, irruption, or furrow. To blaspheme would be to cut oneself off from the object of blasphemy.

"To forgive" can also mean to set free, let go, loosen, leave out, omit, or from the roots, to restore something to its original state.

So from these possibilities, we could compose the following expanded rendering of Matthew 12:31, which attempts to give some of the nuances that Jesus' listeners may have heard:

> *All types of tangled behavior,*
> *the missing and falling,*
> *the rips and tears—*

all the ways you cut yourself off,
break your connection, or
disrupt the pattern—
can and will be mended.
Sooner or later, you will be freed from error,
your mistakes embraced with emptiness,
your arrhythmic action returned to the original beat.
But your state cannot be mended or repaired,
when you cut yourself off from the Source of all rhythm—
the inhaling, the exhaling
of all air, wind, and atmosphere, seen and unseen—
the Holy Breath.

When we "sin against the Holy Spirit," we can only be healed by an involuntary action of surrender that places us back in the sacred communion of Unity. We cannot, of course, actually forget to breathe. We can, however, fail to breathe with a sense of connection to other people and our surroundings. Our current Western culture does not, in fact, encourage us to be aware of our breathing communion with our surroundings. If it did, we would probably have quite a different world than we have today. Yet we can learn to heal our relationships through a deeper experience of breathing.

HONORING THE SACRED BREATH

As Jesus said, "Where your treasure is, there will your heart be also" (Matthew 6:21). We can begin by devoting some time to finding the unique gifts of our own breathing, which is like that of no other human being. We each have our own rhythm, our own way to sense the wave of our breathing as it rises and falls.

Lie or sit comfortably for a few minutes, and again place one hand lightly over the heart. Without trying to change anything, simply notice the breath. There are many different moments in the breath's journey: the feeling of it as it begins to come in, when it approaches fullness, as it briefly turns over, and then when it begins to go out, when it approaches emptiness, and when it turns over again. At each twist and turn of the breath's journey, our bodies respond in a particular way. We may also notice a presence or absence of sensation, thought, or emotion at a particular stage. We may feel that we want to stay longer in one part of the journey than another—the beginning, the middle, or the end.

Simply notice all of these sensations without judgment for a few minutes. If you wish, gradually come back into everyday awareness by drawing freely on paper the feeling of your own breathing wave. This is not a clinical assessment or an art project, but a kind of intuitive snapshot of your feeling of breathing at one moment in time. Perhaps some words and images will also arise.

This type of practice is best done regularly over a period of a month or more. Your drawings and words become a sort of "breath journal," and at the end of the month, they may tell you more about your relationship to breath than any book can. Like a dream journal, as you begin to recognize your own signs and symbols—in this case the signposts on your own breath journey—you can begin to interpret them in light of your own experience. Breathing can become a sort of oracle or barometer that tells us what emotional "weather" will enter our lives.

Such exploration, as also the wisdom implied in the words of Jesus, relates directly to the insights of several body-oriented therapists and psychologists of this century. A primary tenet of all the new therapies, as well as the so-called new physiology can be stated simply: the degree of flexibility of breath in the body not only indicates internal psychic or emotional health, but also the degree of healthy connection to others.[11] From this standpoint, many of the problems of our world today may simply be due to a failure to breathe properly. Or as Jesus said, to a sin against the Holy Breath.

FINDING OUR HOME IN THE BREATH

To allow oneself to breathe with a simple, unencumbered connection to the sacred is not so simple, however. As soon as we begin to breathe consciously, we encounter all of the subtle ways in which we hold our breath.

For instance, in Matthew's version of the Beatitudes (5:3ff), Jesus affirms various conditions in which one finds oneself, and shows how they can lead to a condition of harmony with the Universe. As we shall see in a later chapter, the word for "blessed" that begins each saying can also be translated "ripe." An Aramaic reading of the first three Beatitudes reveals their message as intimately concerned with breathing and with what happens when we begin to breathe more deeply and consciously.

For instance, the translation of the first Beatitude at the beginning of this chapter points to the first step in any deep healing process: the realization that we ultimately have no home or possession except our breathing. When we say that a particular event in our lives has "knocked the wind out of us," we experience this state. When it occurs, then at least for a period of time we begin to breathe more deeply. Deeper breathing can also make us aware of sensations and emotions that we have not been feeling. In fact, we may have been subtly holding our breath in order to avoid feeling them. With this in mind, we can take another look at the second Beatitude, translated in the King James version: "Blessed are they that mourn: for they shall be comforted."

"To mourn"[12] in Aramaic can also mean to be in confusion or turmoil, to wander, literally or figuratively. Certainly many of us have discovered this confusion when we begin to breathe more deeply—for instance, when we have faced our own mortality. "To be comforted" in Aramaic can also mean to be united inside, to return from wandering, or to see the face of what one hopes for.

With these additional meanings, we could do open translations of the second Beatitude like this:

Ripe are those who feel at loose ends,
coming apart at the seams;
they shall be knit back together within.

Blessed are those in turmoil and confusion;
they shall be united inside.

As this follows the saying about breath in the first Beatitude, I believe it suggests a necessary state of confusion that we can "breathe through" and realize as an opportunity to grow more conscious of Sacred Unity. Similarly, in the quote we saw from the Gospel of Thomas in chapter one, Jesus advocates seeking, finding, and being troubled, in order to marvel and then "reign over the All." In another passage from Thomas, he says:

Blessed is the person who has struggled.
He has found life. (Saying 58)

The third Beatitude takes this theme a step further. Here the Aramaic sense of the words is startling compared to the King James translation: "Blessed are the meek: for they shall inherit the earth."

In Aramaic, the word translated as "meek"[13] means literally those who have softened what is rigid. This softening implies a condition both inside and outside us. The phrase "inherit the earth" in Aramaic does not mean to acquire a piece of property. The word for "inherit" also means to receive strength, power, and sustenance. The word for "earth" (*ar'ah*) can also refer to all of nature, as well as to the natural power that manifests through the diversity of beings in the universe.

So a very plausible open translation of this saying, with the Aramaic nuances added, might sound like this:

> *Ripe are those who soften what is rigid, inside and out; they shall be open to receive strength and power—their natural inheritance—from nature.*

The first three Beatitudes tell us that the natural result of conscious breathing is, first, some confusion and turmoil. Then we soften and can begin to absorb universal energy from everywhere around us.

We can again compare these insights to those of various body researchers of this century who have demonstrated conclusively that the idea of the body as a machine is completely inappropriate. The body's movement is not an automatic system of levers and pulleys, but rather a living flow of a whole organism in which awareness plays a very large part. For instance, one can become aware of the sensation of the position in space of joints, muscles, tissues, and organs on a very minute level. These sensations can be sensed and influenced by fine-tuning one's awareness. In this context, the awareness of breathing and the breathing wave can have a powerful therapeutic effect.[14]

BORN AGAIN—REVISITED

If we return now to the final phase of Jesus' conversation with Nicodemus, we see that it contains another beautiful expression of the spiritual life as a life of conscious breathing. To be reborn from the breath by following the sensation of it inside, into the seeming darkness, and out again is the foundation of many Western breathing therapies today. One steps off into the unknown, into what seems like the dark and foreboding place of one's inner emotional life. With perseverance, one comes through to a new state of being.

The last part of Jesus' advice to Nicodemus, which is phrased beautifully (if translated misleadingly) in the King James version, seems to point to such a spiritual awakening. This awakening takes us beyond a world of duality into a communion with all that is:

> *The wind bloweth where it listeth, and thou hearest the sound*
> *thereof, but canst not tell whence it cometh, and whither it goeth;*
> *so is every one that is born of the Spirit.* (John 3:8)

Using many of the nuances of breath and spirit that we have explored so far, we can expand this to:

> *The breath, the wind, and the spirit*
> *obey their own mysterious moods*
> *and their own harmonious laws.*
> *When you hear their voices*
> *and feel their touch,*
> *you know they exist without a doubt.*
> *But you do not understand*
> *how they come together,*
> *how they rise and fall as they*
> *pass over and through the earth.*
>
> *Just as mysterious seems*
> *the movement and the purpose*
> *of every human being*
> *who has returned to the Source*

and been reborn from the Great Dark
through the power of breath and of spirit.

In one of the earliest Jewish mystical practices, the practitioner tried to reexperience the descent of the spirit and breath into form, and then experience resurrection and ascension in a journey of return to the "throne" of the Holy One. This practice related to both the mystery of creation as well as the vision of various prophets.[15] An Aramaic view of Jesus shows us clear links to this tradition. As we shall see in the following chapters, Jesus consistently tried to connect Semitic concepts of holiness, light, kingdom, earth, and heaven with his listeners' personal, often mystical, experience of the sacred, rather than with the conditions of their class, wealth, or ritual purity as defined by the political and religious structures of his day. To take such a stance was both revolutionary and dangerous.

THE BREATH IN ACTION

Each time we feel the wind pass over our skin, we can remember a time when we were only breath. We can also remember when the whole planet was still the germ of an idea in the mind of the Holy One. In the normal business of our everyday lives, this may be too much to ask. In nature, at ease, we are sometimes inspired to such profound contemplation. Even in the city, however, we can learn to breathe in rhythm. By so doing, we can begin to free ourselves from patterns of held breathing that prevent us from uncovering the perfection of our humanity. Here is one suggested body prayer:

While you walk down the street, bring the rhythm of your foot-steps into alignment with the rhythm of your breathing. At first, try inhaling to a count of four and exhaling to a count of four, and use this balanced rhythm to harmonize breathing and walking.

As you proceed, sense the breath more and more in the middle of the chest, in the area near the heart. Feel as though the breath leads you and helps you along, preparing you for what is ahead. At the same time, the awareness of breathing allows you to be more present to the needs of the moment. To help focus, you could also say to yourself the Aramaic words A-la-ha Ru-hau (Unity is Breath) in a rhythm of four. After five to ten minutes, or when you reach your destination, allow yourself to come to standing. Sense your breathing as it returns to whatever its natural rhythm wants to be. In the space of one or two breaths, celebrate the connection of your breath to all that breathes, and to the Sacred Breath itself.

Chapter Four

HOLINESS: CREATING SPACE FOR THE SACRED

Clear holy space around your Name:
let it be the center on which
our life turns.

Focus your light within us—make it useful:
as the rays of a beacon
show the way.

> —alternate readings of the second line of the Lord's Prayer,
> Matthew 6:9, from the Aramaic (KJV: "Hallowed be thy name.")

WHEN WE SPEAK OF WHAT IS SACRED OR HOLY, SUCH AS THE HOLY BREATH, WE PRESUME WE KNOW WHAT WE MEAN. THE WORD "HOLINESS" IN THE WESTERN OR European sense brings up the image of something to do with religion, God, or the powers that administer these concepts. The word for holy used in the Greek Gospels, *hagios*, means anything that induces religious awe. In this concept of holiness, which influences our Western one, a separate subject and object always exist. We hold something outside ourselves in reverence or awe because we presume there are unbridgeable gaps between the divine, humanity, and nature.

In a Middle Eastern cultural framework, where "God" means Unity, the holiness of anything has to do with the extent to which it uniquely participates in this all-pervading Unity. For instance, all breath, air, wind,

and spirit return to one breath—*ruha d'qoodsha*. This Holy Breath ful-
fills its purpose by being the unique essence of breath. Like a clear note
struck by a stringed instrument, Holy Breath gathers all smaller, individual expressions of breath to itself before it returns to the universal
silence.

The word for holy in Aramaic, *qadash*,[1] combines two old Semitic
roots. The first (KD) points to the pivot or point upon which everything
turns. The second (ASh) suggests a circle that unfolds from that point
with power and heat.

To become holy in an Aramaic sense then means to create separate
space for whatever becomes the pivot of our lives, the axis on which our
universe turns. In this way, we clarify the essence of our being so that
we can find our unique place in the cosmic Unity. We fully individu-
ate—which feels like a process of separation—in order to enrich the
whole texture of the reality of Alaha. Our holiness is fulfilled when we
recognize and pursue the purpose of our lives, when we realize our own
"I am." This sense of *qadash* resonates with another saying of Jesus in
the Gospel of Thomas:

> *Cleave a piece of wood, (the) I am is there;*
> *lift up a stone, you will find me there also.* (Saying 77:2-3)

The image of creating space emerges in the two translations of the
Aramaic for "hallowed be thy name" (*nitqadash shmakh*)[2] that begin
this chapter. The image of light comes into the picture as another possible meaning for the word "name," and also relates to the notion of
holiness as spaciousness. When we focus light, we direct its beam
through a lens that realigns the light waves in order to make them more
concentrated. The space around the light beam separates it from other
light that is not focused this way. Likewise, in an oil lantern, the wick is
surrounded by a glass enclosure. Enclosing the light in a separate space
helps focus and magnify it. In the same sense, when we create a sepa-

rate, sacred space for the name, sound, or atmosphere of Sacred Unity, this helps intensify its effects in our lives.

How and where can such a sacred space be created? If we take the meaning outwardly, we can set up a sacred space in our room, home or community. It is the human urge to celebrate communally that has led to the organization of religion in all of its worldwide forms. Some cultures construct special buildings for this purpose. Others continue to realize that the whole of nature, in all of its extravagant uniqueness, should remind us of the sacred.

PRAYER AS SPACE

Ultimately, however, we must each create a personal image of the sacred that leads us toward the ultimate mystery. The first and perhaps most difficult step requires us to leave space for that image to develop. This challenge led the disciples of Jesus to ask, "How should we pray?"

In Aramaic, the word for pray, shela,[3] can mean to incline or bend toward, listen to, or lay a snare for. We lay a snare with our devotion and patiently wait, hoping to catch some inspiration at the right moment. The old Hebrew roots also present the image of a bottomless depth or cavern, or the shadow or shade created by a canopy, roof, or veil. The first image suggests the feeling of depth or spaciousness that prayer should cultivate. We open a space for the feeling of the sacred. The second image of a canopy or veil, again a sculpting of space, indicates the way our image of the sacred provides shade from the more impersonal, uncompromising divine reality that is beyond human images. This idea receives a comment in the Gospel of Thomas:

> The images are visible to humanity,
> but the light within them is hidden in the image
> of the light of the Father.

*This light reveals itself, but the real image
is hidden by this light.* (Saying 83)

Historically, Western culture has not created space very well. Since
the time that it forgot that nature itself is sacred, the West's overwhelming impulse has been to fill space, not create it. If Europeans saw land
that appeared unused or unproductive, they tried to occupy and use it,
even if other people already lived there (as was the case in all the colo-
nized societies of the Americas, Africa, Asia, and Australia). This subconscious push to fill space led to the notion of manifest destiny in
North America and elsewhere. In the modern era, the impulse to make
commercial use of wilderness areas rather than leave them as symbols
of sacred spaciousness arises from the same inner fixation.

We as Westerners, then, should not underestimate the difficulty we
face when we try to cultivate inner space. Western culture has raised us
to feel that any private, personal experience of the divine is somehow
dangerous. Again, the attitude toward the inner wilderness—the unexplored regions of our psyches—mirrors our culture's treatment of the
outer wilderness. The Western entertainment industry metaphorically
fills and colonizes our inner territory with images of its own choosing.

Significantly, the Gospels report that Yeshua prayed and healed
primarily in nature, not inside buildings. In addition, in the majority of
Gospel sayings where Yeshua uses the word "holy," he does so in reference to the Holy Breath, not religious rituals or property. He radically
reoriented the notion of holiness away from buildings, institutions, and
class-based rules, and toward a more personal sense of holiness, as
defined by the Jewish prophets before him.[4]

In the Gospel of Thomas, Yeshua sets up a standard for holiness
that does not eliminate outer codes, but subjects them to a test—the
test of one's inner motivation. His disciples questioned him: "Do you
want us to fast? And how should we pray and give alms? And what diet
should we observe?" And Jesus answered:

Do not lie. And do not do what you hate. For all things are manifest before the face of the Universe. For there is nothing hidden that shall not be revealed and there is nothing covered that shall remain without being uncovered. (Saying 6:1-5)

The Nature of Sacred Space

The following brief meditation may help create a sense of sacred spaciousness.

Find a place outside, in as natural a surrounding as you can. If you cannot see green, growing things, close your eyes and imagine them. Breathe in the oxygen that the natural world gives off in its process of growth. As you exhale, feel your breath return nourishing carbon dioxide to nature. Now focus on the sensation of breathing in the middle of your chest and imagine there a pristine wilderness with all of its vigor and possibility. Feel that the exchange of sacred breath is nourishing both wildernesses— inside and outside. Learning the shape and feeling of our own inner wild spaces may take the same amount of time and effort that learning to survive in the outer wilderness would. An easy, relaxed, and full awareness of breathing—ruha—allows us to explore and value each part of our inner territory, without needing to either plow it under or pave it over.

Space as Creator

The image of sacred space as creative goes back to one of the most ancient streams of Middle Eastern spirituality: the stories about the Egyptian deity Ptah, the guardian of both space and creation who speaks the universe into existence. One of the hymns to Ptah from the third millennium BCE includes this passage about how spaciousness can create:

> All work and crafts,
> the movement of arms and legs,
> every stirring tendril
> conforms to this process of Ptah:
> space unfurls
> heart reveals
> voice clarifies
> life creates.[5]

We take a step toward creating something by leaving the space for it to happen. If we begin to understand holiness as the creation of space, we can reevaluate what is really holy in our lives. What gives us a feeling of expanded possibility? What allows our hearts to reveal what our next steps should be?

PRAYER IN THE CLOSET

These images of holy spaciousness arise in several sayings of Yeshua. When he talks about prayer in Matthew 6:6, he uses the image of a closet or chamber to which one can retreat to pray. The King James version has it:

> But thou, when thou prayest, enter into thy closet, and when thou hast shut thy door, pray to thy Father which is in secret; and thy Father which seeth in secret shall reward thee openly.

Here again, we can examine the Aramaic roots of some key words in order to uncover deeper layers of this statement, in which Jesus turns the tables on a popular conception of prayer in his time: public prayer for the purpose of increasing one's social status. We have already viewed some of the possible images that the word "prayer" presents: a hollowed space, a snare, a veil that produces a shadow. The ranges of meaning in Aramaic of four other words in this passage enhance these images.

The word translated as "closet"[6] suggests through its primary root a sign, symbol, or story that reveals something else behind it. The closet need not be only, or even primarily, a physical inner space, but can also be an emotional and spiritual one.

The word for "door" has the same root as that for "opening" (*ptah*), which we have already seen. It can mean an opening between various "worlds" of one's existence.

The Aramaic word for "secret" comes from a verb that can mean to veil or protect. This word is also used to refer to inner sight in Aramaic. The word for "openly" can also mean that which is revealed by being manifested in form. The roots of this word suggest the swell of the ocean as it builds up slowly and then reveals itself in an expansive, forceful movement.

So an expansion of the above passage, with the nuances available in Aramaic added, provides this rendering:

> *When you want to lay yourself open for the divine,*
> *like a snare that is hollowed out to its depth,*
> *like a canopy that projects a shadow*
> *from the divine heat and light*
> *into your soul,*
> *then go into your inner place,*
> *to that story or symbol that reminds you of the sacred.*
> *Close the doors of your awareness to*
> *the public person you think yourself to be.*
> *Pray to the parent of creation with your inner sense,*
> *the outer senses turned within.*

Veiling yourself, the mystery may be unveiled through you.
By opening yourself to the flow of the sacred,
somewhere, resounding in some inner form,
the swell of the divine ocean can move through you.
The breathing life of all reveals itself
in the way you live your life.

In the Aramaic, this passage presents a multilayered image. We focus on some center, image, or feeling that presents the sacred to our inner being. If we give our awareness space, inner and outer, to contemplate this sacred center, we expand beyond who we think ourselves to be and allow the sacred to manifest through our own being.

Sacred Commitment

To create space for the sacred is one part of the equation. To choose an image, ideal, or goal representing the sacred upon which to focus is another. Today, with all we know of the historical abuses of organized religion, many people are understandably reluctant to commit to any kind of dogma, myth, image, or ideal. In fact, the whole notion of idealism has fallen out of favor in preference for a view that everything changes and nothing carries any inherent meaning. This is a climate in which buying and selling become the highest good.

This point of view ignores the fact that the human relationship to nature has not ultimately changed. We are still dependent upon air for breath, earth for food, and sunlight for the source of our energy. In the view of a Middle Eastern spirituality, the whole natural world reveals a greater Mystery behind it, which is beyond name and form. The human relationship to that ultimate Mystery has also not changed. While certain religious symbols may have exhausted their meaning, we can return to the same source from which the prophets and mystics of the past drew them: the human relationship to breath, nature, and the great Mystery.

When we consciously commit ourselves to a goal—in prayer, meditation, or action—we make a spiritual statement. We are leaving space for the One to speak to us through whatever happens in the course of our meditation or endeavor. The way we ask makes a difference. This is made clear in Jesus' words in Matthew 7:7 (KJV: "Ask, and it shall be given you; seek, and ye shall find; knock, and it shall be opened unto you").

All three words that ask us to exert ourselves—"ask," "seek," and "knock"[7]—in Aramaic reflect the sense of creating space with sincere intensity. All of the results of these efforts—"given," "find," and "opened"—in Aramaic emphasize processes of nature that happen easily, such as a loving action or a natural response to something that has already happened. When we work up the passion to follow something wholeheartedly, we blow into life the fire of love within us. This devotion, rather than the object we pursue, is the real goal.

In the end, it doesn't so much matter where we start as *that* we start. Holiness is about wholeness. When we allow something to be sacred for us, to remind us of the ultimate mystery, that some-thing can take us to every thing. It is, again, a conscious remembrance of the breath as holy that guides us on our journey.

Jesus as the Way

We have spoken of nature, images, symbols, and goals as guides toward our inner sense of holiness, but what about a holy person—in this case, Jesus himself? This idea can be problematic to many, because of the interpretation by some branches of Western Christianity that "Jesus is the only way." This attitude helped fuel Western missionary and colonial efforts in the past century.

In reevaluating these exclusive claims, a number of Christian theologians of this century have promoted the necessity of what is called the "pluralist imperative."[8] As this opinion goes, in a world of many cultures, it behooves Christians to read their own texts more selectively and emphasize the wisdom elements of the message, in distinction to the more exclusivist elements. These theologians point out that the diversity in attitudes among the Gospel writers themselves, both in the way they report Jesus' sayings and actions and in what they actually report, should encourage diversity within Christian thought itself, as well as encourage acceptance of the differences between Christians and people of other faiths.[9]

In addition, the earliest strands of the Gospels (for instance, sayings sources like Q and the Gospel of Thomas) show us a Jesus who places little or no emphasis on belief in himself in order to be saved. Instead, he emphasizes a radical change of heart and life according to the cultivation of wisdom. For this reason, a number of Christian biblical scholars advocate that the more exclusivist passages attributed to Jesus, like "I am the way, the truth, and the life," should be taken in the sense of what one calls "love language": appropriate for those within a particular faith community, but not applicable for those outside of it.[10]

If we are to find any wisdom sense in these more exclusivist passages, we must look again to the Aramaic to see if the subtext can reveal a deeper layer. For instance, we can look at the passage quoted above from John 14:6 (KJV):

> I am the way, the truth, and the life:
> No man cometh unto the Father, but by me.

In the Aramaic version, we find the construction "I am" represented by the word "I" repeated: *ena ena*,[11] as in "I-I." This has several possible interpretations: an intensive form of "I," the essence of individuality, the "I" inside the "I," or something like "the 'I am.'" Again, in a culture where the word for God means Unity, the sense of the individual cannot be ultimately separated from the divine. Only one "I Am" exists, which is Alaha.

The Aramaic word *urha*, usually translated "way," is related to one of the words for light (which we will consider in the next chapter). Here it is the light that uncovers a path, shows a hidden possibility, or reveals a practical way that was previously unknown.

The word *sherara*, usually translated as "truth," is the same that we considered in the passage about spirit and truth in chapter three. It points to a solution or to liberation, the opening of a circle, the sense of right direction that is in harmony with the universe.

The word *hayye*, usually translated "life," indicates in both Aramaic and Hebrew the sacred life force, the primal energy that pervades all of nature and the universe.

The phrase "but by me" is made up of three prepositions in Aramaic (plus the word-ending meaning "me").[12] The first, "except," can also mean "if only" and "although." Thus the word expresses a condition that passes away, like the body. For this reason, it is related to the word for mourning the dead.

The second, a word that appears only in the Aramaic version and means "if" or "provided that," expresses a sense of present time, that is, what exists now.

Finally, we find the preposition "by" in Aramaic prefixed as the letter *b*. This frequently used preposition can express many different relationships: through, in, among, with, at, to, into, on, by, for, or because. What unites these various meanings is the action of something passing from interior to exterior, or from idea to form.

Together, the three prepositions suggest a process that (1) recognizes that forms pass away; (2) makes use of forms in the present, to create a sense of presence; and (3) recognizes that forms provide a vehicle from one reality to another. So we could render the passage like this:

The "I Am" is the path,
the sense of right direction and
the life force to travel it.
Simple presence illuminates what's ahead,
frees our choices,
and connects us to nature's power.
No one comes into rhythm with
the breathing life of all,
the sound and atmosphere
that created the cosmos,
except through the
breathing, sound, and atmosphere,
of another embodied "I"
connected to
the ultimate "I Am."

In this sense, the person of Jesus, whom his disciples see and who walks, talks, and eats with them, provides a doorway between the realities. Through his presence they can find a personal relationship with *abwoon*, the breathing life of all. Through attunement to Jesus' breathing, atmosphere, and way of prayer, they will be led to experience what he experiences. Focusing on the teacher as a doorway to the divine is a spiritual practice that still exists today in Jewish and Islamic mysticism.

Perhaps I am stretching the point here. One could simply say, with the Christian theologians mentioned above, that the phrase "except through" is only valid for those for whom Jesus is the primary guide or touchstone for their spirituality. Nonetheless, the consistent images in the passage point to an actual spiritual practice that uses rhythm, vibration, and breathing as doors to a more complete sense of Sacred Unity. I believe that Saying 108 from the Gospel of Thomas points to this practice as well:

Whoever drinks from my mouth shall become as I am, and I myself will become he, and the hidden things shall be revealed to him.

FINDING THE HOLY CENTER

It is possible to pursue any goal with concentration and awareness of breath and allow this pursuit to become holy. No doubt, when engaged in everyday life it is easier to forget this than when we are surrounded by the awe-inspiring qualities of nature. Here the notion of spiritual practice enters: We practice remembrance until we forget forgetfulness, to paraphrase one Sufi proverb.

Return for a moment to the awareness of the heart as sacred nature. How much diversity, wildness, and beauty can it hold? And what does the holding? Can we allow a feeling of "center" to develop, by sensing our breath and the beating of our heart? Can this center embrace everything that has arisen in the universe since the original, primeval fireball?

As you hold this feeling, using it as a touchstone, focus on a symbol or image that is sacred to you, perhaps one that represents a practical goal you have for your life. Imbue this symbol with the passion of your devotion. Allow for the possibility that as you pursue this goal, you will make space in your life for the divine to enter. Open the space inside that will allow the One to bring the blessing of whatever relationship, knowledge, or work is in your destiny to experience.

Chapter Five

FACES OF LIGHT: VIBRATION AND GUIDANCE

Wherever two or three gather
in my name and light,
in my experience of
the vibrating, shining cosmos—
then the "I Am" is already there
around, among, and inside them.

—alternative reading from the Aramaic of Matthew 18:20
(KJV: "For where two or three are gathered together
in my name, there am I in the midst of them.")

WHILE OUR WESTERN LANGUAGES HAVE ONLY ONE WORD EACH FOR LIGHT AND DARKNESS, SEMITIC LANGUAGES HAVE SEVERAL WORDS, AS WELL AS VERY DIFFERENT CONcepts about them. In Greek and European thought, we have a simple split between the two words. In Aramaic, we find different qualities of light and darkness, as well as the recognition of a continuum between them. Especially in Western religious thought, we usually find the implication that light is always good and darkness always bad. Semitic thought recognizes the value and limitations of both qualities.

The first face of light we consider is the Aramaic word usually translated "name" (which we saw in the possessive form in "hallowed be thy name" in the previous chapter). The root word of this family, *shem*,[1] can mean light, word, sound, reputation, name, and atmosphere. The roots themselves indicate the space or movement extending from a point (Sh) that defines some specific form of existence (M). What unifies these meanings is the idea of vibration: everything that vibrates its way into existence as a seemingly separate being carries its own unique *shem*. As you may have already anticipated, all individual name-light-vibrations return in various ways to the one sacred *shem* of the divine, which is beyond human words or names. All vibration is part of the whole vibration of the universe. In fact, one of the words for "universe" or "cosmos" in Hebrew-Aramaic consists of the root *shem* along with the ending -*aya*, which indicates that the divine name-light-vibration is in every particle of existence. Some of those additional senses of the word usually translated as "heaven" informed my renditions of the first line of the prayer of Jesus in chapter one.

Since this face of light can mean both sound and vibration, one could also hear the second line of the prayer Jesus gave, usually translated "hallowed be thy name," in these additional ways:

Make your one Voice the center
of our lives, hallowed in every
sound we hear.

All vibrating waves return to one ocean
and to You, the nameless, creative One
behind it.

If we unravel this a bit more, we can see the embodied sense behind this concept of name-light. When a baby is born, it has its own particular, pure atmosphere. The gaze of an infant fills us with a light that seems to come from another world. In many ancient cultures, an infant was often given a name that expressed the particular light, atmosphere, or feeling that she or he brought into existence. Likewise, in Jewish, Islamic, and some Christian contemplative traditions, one may receive a new name, emphasizing a particular quality, at a certain point in one's spiritual journey.

"IN MY NAME"

If we bring this understanding of *shem* into the dozens of passages in the Gospels where Jesus mentions praying, healing, or asking for something "in my name" or "in the name of God," we can hear a much expanded sense of the words. The translation of Matthew 18:20 that begins this chapter explores this. Keeping in mind that the preposition "in" (*b*) can also mean within, along with, among, or from within, "in my name" can also mean:

With my atmosphere . . .

From within my experience . . .

In rhythm with my sound . . .

With my sense of illumination . . .

With the light of my essence . . .

From within my name . . .

No doubt the use of Jesus' name in Christian prayers conveys to the devotee a vibrational sense of his being. The name *Yeshua* itself, from which the Greek-English *Jesus* is derived, means: The One Nameless Being (*Yah*) saves or restores (*shua*). This name affirms a reality greater than the individual person of Jesus yet also includes his particular presence.

When he used the phrase "in my name," I feel that Jesus again pointed to the Middle Eastern spiritual practice of prayer or healing through attunement to the atmosphere of a particular holy person. This practice can bring one into direct relationship with Sacred Unity. One can also come into such a direct relationship immediately; however, most traditions provide for a more gradual method as well. By attuning to the rhythm of a person who has "been there before," one can receive the impression of an experience with much more certainty. The whole notion of apprenticeship common in many ancient traditions relies upon this principle.

Two statements in the Gospel of Thomas also seem to point to this practice. The first emphasizes the value of the teacher:

> Look upon the living as long as you live, so that you will not die, seeking to see him, and be unable to see. (Saying 59)

The second emphasizes the value of the presence of the teacher as a door to an experience that transcends personal presence:

> I will give you what eye has not seen and what ear has not heard and what hand has not touched and what has not arisen in the heart of humanity. (Saying 17)

We can also recognize that the idea of spirituality in older cultures and traditions emphasizes relationship and community more than our own. What we call personal growth could even be seen as egocentric in this light.[2] As we shall see, one can achieve a balance between the individual and the communal that expresses the balance that existed between earth and heaven "in the beginning."

DARKNESS SHINES

I want to emphasize that the *shem*-light includes all vibration, from the slowest to the fastest, from the most dense waves to the most expanded. It includes what we normally call darkness, and what physicists now call "dark matter," the stuff that makes up most of what we know as the universe.

The notion of darkness shining is a paradox in Western thought, but not in Middle Eastern. It finds another expression in the Hebrew word *kevod*, which is usually translated as "glory," but can also mean weight or esteem. The roots of this word suggest a force of vibration that acts from within the densest center of every being. Isaiah's vision of the song of the angels around the heavenly throne—a hymn used in the Christian liturgy as the Sanctus—expresses this sense of "heavy glory" linked with the healing power of *kadosh*, or spaciousness (KJV: Holy, holy, holy, is the Lord of Hosts: the whole earth is full of his glory).[3]

The experience of *shem* connects one through sound and vibration to other living creatures and to the whole cosmos. Any meditation or spiritual practice that uses sound can help us make this connection. The key is to maintain awareness of the sound within the body itself. Because we are not generally taught to recognize our own bodies as temples of God,[4] or to feel the holiness of their vibrations, it is easy for spiritual practice using sound (or light) to become disembodied. If one loses the awareness of the so-called physical body and yet remains conscious, this experience may help one realize that more exists to life than simply the physical. Yet repeated experiences of this type do not help bridge the worlds: light and dark, body and spirit become split apart too easily. This split lies at the root of much of the religious fanaticism that we see around us.

Begin this practice by finding a place of relative peace, preferably in nature. Relax into the sensation of your breathing. Again place one hand lightly over the chest and feel the rise and fall of the breath there. Notice whether you can feel any sensation of the heartbeat and, behind that, of other pulsations of the body. Perhaps your stomach growls. Or you can feel your skin itch, or the breath as it enters your nose, throat, and lungs. Behind all these there may lie more subtle pulsations, for instance the slow pulsation of fluid up and down the spine, bathing the brain in mois-

ture. Do not regard any of these sensations as distractions from the meditation. Instead, regard them as expressions of shem— the name, light, vibration of the sacred.

As each sensation arises, use the awareness of the breath to illuminate it, that is, to feel it consciously and clearly. As you do so, breathe the sound and feeling of shema *toward it, connecting the feeling or sensation with that of nature around you. Sooner or later, find yourself in the middle of one vibrating universe.*

If you are unable to be in nature, sit quietly wherever you may be and consider every sensation within, every vibration out-side—even what you would normally call noise—as an expression of the vibrating cosmos.

THE FIRST LIGHT AND DARK

Before we look at the other word besides *shema* that Jesus used for light, we have to backtrack a bit to the Jewish creation story in Genesis, in order to see how it uses the terms "darkness" and "light."

Just like Aramaic, the biblical Hebrew in Genesis is open to multi-layered interpretations. One can always draw more from the Hebrew of the Genesis story. This has occupied various commentators in the rab-binical tradition for centuries, and this is what motivates the tradition of *midrash*, or interpretive commentary. As with any mythic story, the cre-ation story in Genesis is expressed in symbolic language. According to one reading, the whole first part of the story happens first in the realm of cosmic idea or archetype, then proceeds to manifestation. One mean-ing of the Hebrew word for "in the beginning" expresses archetypal time, a "beginning-ness" that precedes linear time as measured on earth.[5]

According to the story, darkness (*hoshech*), which is mentioned in Genesis 1:2, is older than light, which doesn't appear until verse three.

This darkness is also an essential part of the creation story. The roots of the Hebrew word suggest a violent, disordered, chaotic movement, or an inner force that tries to extend itself out of harmony with its surroundings. As Jewish mystics came to use the word, it expresses everything that is dense and unknowable from the human standpoint. Like the violent and chaotic acts of nature we experience today, this type of energy struck fear into the hearts of human beings. Yet this imbalance itself seems to be a necessary part of the story.

In the case of the Genesis story, the great archetypal darkness-chaos drew toward itself the breath of the Universe Being (KJV: "and darkness was upon the face of the deep. And the Spirit of God moved upon the face of the waters"). The Hebrew words give rise to the image of this breath interpenetrating, inspiring, and animating the darkness.[6]

This intimacy gives birth to the creation of light in verse three, the well-known, "Let there be light: and there was light" of the King James version. The Hebrew word used here for light, *aor*, refers to all varieties of illuminating intelligence, which move in straight, harmonious lines, not like the curves and swirls of the older darkness.

In addition, the Hebrew word translated as "let there be" is the same as the one translated as "there was." Hebrew presents the concept, paradoxical to Western minds, that future and past are connected. If "light shall be" also means "light was," then in some sense the call of the future ignites the reality of the past in the opportunity of the present.

Now some of this may seem a bit abstract until we consider the way in which our human intelligence actually makes sense of our lives. For instance, I may have experienced something in the past that seems to have absolutely no reason or purpose. No cause and effect seems to be operating, and I learned nothing from the experience. It seems random, disordered, chaotic. It might have been experienced as violent, even if not physically so. It is only later in life that another experience brings sense to what happened in the past, or shows me that I did actually learn or undergo something then that is needed now. Sometimes what I learned is empathy for another in a similar situation.

If we place too much focus on either future or past, we may miss the opportunity of the present. Nevertheless, we can hear the future call to the past in the same way that the sun, rain, and warmth of spring call to the seed sleeping in the earth and awaken it to bloom.

A Balance of Light and Dark

The light of *aor* that awakens and makes sense of existence is called *nuhra*[7] in the Aramaic of Jesus. We can compare this light with the darkness of *hoshech* as we would compare two different but complementary forces, like the straight rays of sunlight and the swirling energies of cloud and wind. Psychologically, they are like the start-to-finish, cause-and-effect nature of rational thinking compared to the zig-zag nature of intuitive thinking.

On one level, what we see in the Genesis story reflects the resolution of a conflict between these two modes of knowing, thinking, and being: the newer, straight-line type of revelation, which is typified by a ray of light that shines on an individual, and the older, curved, instinctual type of revelation, which is embedded in an intuitive, communal understanding of the natural world. In this story, the two are still in balance. Light does not replace darkness.

In fact, Genesis gives both a place in the unfolding creation as day and night. In Hebrew, the word "day" (*iom*) gives scope for unfolding, expanding purpose, like a story that proceeds from event to event. "Night" (*lailah*) allows for assimilation and consolidation, which follow a more mysterious course, like our dream life. We could regard these concepts of day and night as deep insights into the natural world, resulting from close observation of plants and animals on the part of people we normally call primitive.

On another level, the Genesis creation myth describes psychological and spiritual processes. If we form an image and feeling of the sacred in our meditation, we begin to enter "in-the-beginning" time. If we breathe into what seems to be darkness inside, we begin to distinguish—and bring light to—different sensations and different voices in ourselves. Various types of Western psychotherapy and dreamwork focus their work this way. When we gain greater knowledge of this "inner wilderness," a ray of light may enter that makes sense of the whole territory—not just our conscious thoughts, but also what lay hitherto unconscious or subconscious.

To the extent that psychotherapy, meditation, and religious ritual ignore these natural—that is, based on nature—principles of transformation, they are doomed to failure. To escape into light is no better than to continually rummage in darkness. Both light and dark are needed.

The Light under a Bushel

We find a profound use of these archetypes from Genesis in the sayings of Jesus. The image of consciousness or light entering the darkness reappears. Luke and Matthew both report what many scholars consider a very historical saying of Jesus, which in Luke's version begins like this (KJV):[8]

> *No man, when he hath lighted a candle, putteth it in a secret place, neither under a bushel, but on a candlestick, that they which come in may see the light.* (Luke 11:33)

Here Jesus begins in the style of a parable. Considered first on the cultural level, poorer families in first-century Palestine often lived communally in one large single-room dwelling that housed as many as fifty people. Each family would have its own area and its own lamp-holder that would shine light there. If a poor family ran out of lamp oil, they might have to depend on a neighboring family for light. A generous family would not hoard its light. But arguments were possible because light tends to spread without limits.[9]

To find another level of meaning in this saying, we can look at the various Aramaic words used. The word for "lamp" or "candle"[10] comes from a verb that means to be illuminated, imagine, or dream. The word's roots point to a visionary state in which a person's boundaries or sense of self may expand greatly.

The various words used for light in this passage all come from the Aramaic *nuhra*. The same root (NR) also composes the word for "candlestick" or "lampstand" (*menarta*)—the additional prefix *m* indicates the embodiment or materialization of a particular quality or thing.

The word for "bushel" is the name for a dry measure scoop used at the time, but can also indicate any round enclosure. The word for "secret place" is the same one we encountered in the saying on prayer in the previous chapter. It can also mean any veil or shelter, and points to "inner sight" or to things that are ineffable or mystical.

If we take all this into account, we have a parable about being generous not only with physical light, but also with intellectual and spiritual light. If you receive a vision that illuminates circumstances, you naturally share it. If you keep it to yourself, you either suffocate the flame for want of breath, or you keep it veiled in your inner life. You can only do the latter for so long, however, without denying the reality of the vision. We are also generous with illumination when we allow it to penetrate all parts of our being. Then we embody the light fully and put it into practice.

THE EYE AND THE LIGHT

Immediately after telling this parable, Jesus makes its personal— what we might call mystical—meaning more clear (KJV):

The light of the body is the eye: therefore when thine eye is single,
thy whole body also is full of light. (Luke 11:34a)

The Aramaic word used here for "eye" is a complex one.[11] It can mean look, view, opinion, appearance, face, or the surface of something that expresses an inner essence. The word for "single" can also mean upright, stretched out, innocent, sincere, or straightforward. The word used here for "body" can also mean corpse or flesh—the purely physical stuff of a human being, without the living breath.

So we could translate this section of the verse as follows:

The degree of your illumination—
your understanding of all that is—
shines through your eyes, your face,
and all you do.
When your expression is straight and expansive,
without holding back,
like light through a clear lens,
then everything you embody
shows the same flash of intelligence
that helped create the world.

In other words, without being illuminated by *nuhra*, the light of intelligence, the body is just flesh, a corpse. More specifically, Jesus' listeners showed by the light in their eyes the degree to which they consciously understood his teaching.

In the next section of the verse, Jesus continues (KJV):

but when thine eye is evil,
thy body also is full of darkness. (Luke 11:34b)

The word for "evil"[12] in Aramaic means unripe or not at the right time, and is one we shall investigate more fully in chapter nine. The word for "darkness"(*heshuka*) is the Aramaic equivalent of the word for darkness used in Genesis (*hoshech*). So an expanded reading of this sentence could be:

> *But when your expression is veiled,*
> *the eye cloudy and darting,*
> *the action at the wrong time and place,*
> *what you embody of light and understanding*
> *will be chaotic, swirling, obscure.*
> *Your non-understanding then*
> *participates in the primal darkness of the cosmos.*

An obscured gaze shows that a lesson or teaching—light—is not understood consciously. If something is received subconsciously, this may not be reflected in one's expression or action. The rules of the sub-conscious, like the primal darkness of *hoshech*, are obscure, indirect, and circular. For a teaching to reach this level of understanding—for the light to reach the darkness—indirect methods, like parables and stories, are traditionally used in the Middle East.

As the passage continues, it becomes more puzzling in its usual translations (here, KJV):

> *Take heed therefore that the light which is in thee be not dark-*
> *ness.* (Luke 11:35)

Here the Aramaic version gives a more subtle reading. The word usually translated "therefore"[13] can also mean perhaps, unless, or "it may be." It points out a special circumstance that amends what has been said before. The word "not" does not appear in either the Aramaic or Greek text of Luke. So two other hearings of this phrase can be:

> *Take care in this circumstance:*
> *when the light in you actually becomes darkness,*
> *then it is no longer light:*
> *when your understanding loses its clarity*

or becomes lost in complexity,
it cannot claim to be teaching or illumination.

Pay attention that you use clear understanding
for what is straightforward, able to be taught.
Use veiling and darkness for what
is circular, indirect, only able to be suggested.

This calls to mind another saying of Jesus (KJV): "Behold, I send you forth as sheep in the midst of wolves: be ye therefore wise as serpents, and harmless as doves" (Matthew 10:16). The word for "wise" is related to the methods of Hokhmah, Holy Wisdom, which operate in the darkness. We will explore this more in chapter seven. The word for "harmless"[14] can also mean straightforward, sincere, or complete.

In the last segment of this passage in Luke, Jesus suggests that the guidance one experiences as illumination can entirely fill one's being, if the darkness is ready to receive it. In the King James version:

If thy whole body therefore be full of light, having no part dark,
the whole shall be full of light, as when the bright shining of a
candle doth give thee light. (Luke 11:36)

Using the expanded meanings of words we have already seen, we can hear the following nuances of the Aramaic version:

If light comes fully into darkness,
if illumination reaches the depths
of your flesh and soul,
then vibrating, swirling obscurity
marries radiant, straightforward clarity.
"Let there be light" becomes your experience.
For a candle to give illumination,
every part of it must participate:
the dark of the wick

the light of the flame
and the aura of heat.[15]

As we move into the second half of this book, we will return to the darkness of the subconscious and learn what other tools the sayings of Jesus recommend to explore and transform it. The illumination of *nuhra*—working in the light and toward what some traditions call enlightenment—operates by straight-line methods. The work of indirect transformation—"endarkenment"—operates by curved methods. St. John of the Cross called his experience of the latter type of spiritual work "the dark night of the soul." In our lives we are constantly working to make sense of both these "universes" and to integrate them in our everyday lives.

A MEDITATION ON LIGHT AND DARK

For a few moments, gaze at a candle flame and see clearly all three parts of it: the substance and wick that burn, the visible light, and the shimmering wave of heat around the flame. Then allow your eyes to close and visualize the three parts inside you. Each supports the others in order to allow the light of your being to radiate. Use the sensation of the breath to acknowledge the parts of your being that feel the most expansive, that carry your clearest sense of guidance. Use the sensation of the breath to acknowledge those parts deepest inside, which feel the most compressed, chaotic, and unresponsive. As you complete the meditation, hold in your awareness the feeling of the whole candle, rather than its literal image. Acknowledge and give thanks for the way that both the dark and light aspects of your being have brought you to this place in life. Affirm the possibility of a marriage of darkness and light.

Chapter Six

THE REIGN OF UNITY: VISION PLUS "I CAN!"

Turn again!
Return to unity with Unity,
like the sea flowing back to the shore
in ebb tide.
The empowering vision,
the "I Can" of the cosmos,
the reign of all that vibrates,
the queendom of heaven
arrives at this moment!
It draws near, touching us,
carrying us away,
wrenching us back into rhythm
with the vibration of the One.

> —alternative reading of Matthew 3:2 and 4:17,
> words attributed to both John and Jesus
> (KJV: "Repent ye: for the kingdom of heaven is at hand.")

I N THE FOUR GOSPELS JESUS USES THE WORD USUALLY TRANSLATED "KINGDOM" MORE THAN A HUNDRED TIMES, MOST OF THESE IN MATTHEW AND LUKE. NO OTHER WORD THAT JESUS USED HAS been subject to so much speculation. Much of this has centered on whether the kingdom he had in mind was to be earthly or heavenly. Did he intend to set up a select group of devotees who would receive their reward later? Was he advocating a political revolution? Was he predicting the imminent end of the world? Did he change his mind about whether the kingdom was here and now, or later and somewhere else? Was the kingdom supposed to be "within" or "among"? Why did he use so many obscure parables to try to describe it to his students?

First, the word usually translated as "kingdom" is gendered feminine in both Aramaic (*malkuta*)[1] and Hebrew (*mamlaka*). In fact, the word translated as "kingdom" in the Greek New Testament, *basileia*, is also a feminine-gendered noun. Quite apart from any considerations of political correctness, "queendom" would be a more accurate translation. As we now know from archeological records, queens historically preceded kings in the Middle East, as in many other parts of the world. It is not surprising that the gender of the word for their realm reflects this. Second, beyond the issue of gender, the word's roots point to a fully formed (M) extension of power (L) that is centralized and determined (K). This root—MLK—is the sign of the creative word, the empowering vision, the counsel that rules by its ability to express the most obvious next step for a group. On a personal level, this root expresses that which says "I can!" to life.

For thousands of years before there were queens (or kings) in the Middle East, most people traveled nomadically and lived in clans, or large extended family groups. The leaders of these clans were likely to be those who, by their vision and wisdom, could say "I can" on behalf of their communities—for instance, to guide them at the right times and to the right places to graze animals or gather food. I suspect that the ancient Semitic word that became *malkuta* in Aramaic evolved in this way.[2] In one of the Canaanite languages, a word based on the same root—*malkatu*—became a title that honored the Great Goddess.

REPENTANCE AND THE QUEENDOM

The first occurrences of *malkuta* in the Gospels put the same sentence in the mouth of both John the Baptist and Jesus after his temptation in the wilderness. It is usually translated (KJV): "Repent ye: for the kingdom of heaven is at hand." I have translated this saying in an expanded fashion at the beginning of this chapter. The other two other key words also deserve some attention and help illuminate the sense of *malkuta*.

First, the word usually translated "repent"[3] can also mean to return, come again, flow back, or ebb. Its roots show something that turns or returns (T), as though in a circle or spiral, to its origin or to its original rhythm (AB). In a Hebrew-Aramaic sense, to repent means to unite with something by affinity, because it feels like going home.

Second, the word translated "at hand" can also mean to touch, arrive, seize, or bring near.[4] It refers to something happening *now*, in the present, with an almost violent immediacy. The same word is sometimes used with the connotation "to join in battle."

Saying 51 in the Gospel of Thomas conveys a similar sense of immediacy:

> *His disciples said to him: "When will the repose of the dead come about and when will the new world come? He said to them: What you are waiting for has already come, but you do not realize it.*

The Gospels do portray both John and Jesus as having this passionate sense of immediacy. Both prophets link an imminent empowerment of the sacred with the need to return to right timing, rhythm, and harmony with the cosmos. We do not usually connect this sense of timeliness, of turning and returning, with our sense of the word "repent," which is more often associated with conversion to a particular belief or creed. As we shall see later, the word for "repent" is related by root to the word meaning good or blessedly ripe. To return to right rhythm with the sacred leads to a state of being blessed. In this sense, every moment can be a sacred moment, if is in time with Alaha.[5]

THE QUEENDOM—BOTH WITHIN AND AMONG

As I mentioned in chapter two, the arrival of the reign of empowerment that Jesus predicted could be seen as both personal and political. Without a communal change of heart, nonviolent revolution would not be possible. Unless the whole community said "I can!" to a new sense of itself, change would not happen. This reading of *malkuta* illuminates the saying of Jesus in Luke 17:21, usually translated "the kingdom of God is within you," but sometimes "the kingdom of God is among you."

The ambiguity in this passage (and the failure of most translators to deal with it accurately) arises from the fact that the word *entos* found in the Greek New Testament can mean both "within" and "among." The Aramaic preposition *men* offers the same paradox and can stand for both "within" and "among." In its version of the saying in Coptic, the Gospel of Thomas keeps the paradox and renders the saying: "The kingdom is inside of you and outside of you" (Saying 3:3).

We have already seen that the way we experience the inner self—the inner community of voices—can correspond to the way we experience the outer community. While this idea may seem like psychology to us, this is because we as Westerners have been raised to see individuality and community, as well as humanity and nature, as separate. We think that when we give different names to fields like psychology, sociology, or ecology, we actually put definable boundaries around our inner self, our community life, and our relationship with nature. Previous cultures were not so inflated with the idea of control, or so disconnected from their environments.

When we look more closely at the Aramaic version of the passage in Luke, we find some additional shades of meaning for *malkuta*. The King James version reads this way:

> And when he was demanded of the Pharisees, when the kingdom of God should come, he answered them and said, The kingdom of God cometh not with observation: Neither shall they say, Lo here! or, lo there! for, behold, the kingdom of God is within you. (Luke 17:20-21)

The Aramaic word translated as "observation"[6] comes from a verb that means to guard, preserve, or watch something, either physically or mentally—that is, by preserving it in memory.

The Aramaic version of Luke actually uses two prepositions to express a range of meanings beyond what the Greek *entos* (translated as "within" or "among") can offer. These words are *legau men*.[7] The first derives from a word that means inside, inward, or the belly, and can refer to the viscera of an individual or a community. The second word can mean within, among, from, out of, at, on, or by—a range of relationships that all point to the image or definite outline of a being, its "mien" in the antique English usage. Placed together, the two Aramaic words indicate a process that happens "from inside out," or as an inner community expresses itself outwardly. So another way to hear Jesus' response to the Pharisees might be:

> The reign of empowerment you look for
> does not come from watching outside,
> from waiting for it to happen,
> from guarding property, status, or wealth.
> It will not come by pointing to something
> or someone outside yourself.
> The "I Can" of Oneness that will free you
> comes from inside out,
> from an agreement deep in the belly.

*Then your inner community
expresses itself as the face of
powerful and overwhelming unity.*

A parallel passage in the Gospel of Thomas also seems to preserve some sense of movement from inside to outside: "The kingdom . . . is spread out upon the earth and people do not see it" (Saying 113:2).

What Jesus advocated may seem very idealistic. It is nothing less than a wholesale change of heart. This begins in one's interior community of voices as empowerment or faith, and extends outward to overwhelming agreement in the outer community. Such powerful nonviolent revolutions, where a whole community says "enough!" and change happens overnight, are relatively rare in the world's history. Two examples in recent memory are the fall of the Berlin Wall and the ending of apartheid in South Africa. The alternative is more common: one generation's oppressors are replaced by another's, under different names or political parties, but essentially using the same methods and with the same results.

Looking at the long view of things, perhaps Jesus was not an idealist but a pragmatist. His predictions of impending judgment and cataclysm unless a wholesale change of heart occurred seem justified by the events after his crucifixion. Twice within a century—in 66-73 CE and again in 132-136 CE—the Romans put down armed rebellions in Palestine, with tremendous suffering on the part of the poor. Various factions of the people of Palestine fought each other as much as they fought the Romans. In 70 CE the Romans completely destroyed the Jerusalem Temple, the symbol of Jewish status and privilege that various groups had tried to claim, and a war tax was imposed upon all people in the Roman Empire identifiable as Jewish—including Jewish Christians. In 136 CE, the entire city of Jerusalem was destroyed, and a Hellenistic city was built next to it. Access to Jerusalem was forbidden to everyone who looked like a native Judaean. We need look no further for the fulfillment of the various apocalyptic statements attributed to Jesus. In the absence of a communal change of heart, the judgment day had come.[8]

ASKING FOR THE "I CAN" TO COME

The first steps toward the creation of wholehearted empowerment in our lives are to leave space for it and ask for it with sincerity. We can't overlook the power of devotion to create the feeling of possibility in our lives. As we touched upon in chapter four, this seemingly outer devotion also opens doors to our inner community of voices—in Aramaic terms, the *naphsha*[9] or subconscious soul-self. It is there that we find the seeds of *malkuta*—empowerment, the inner revolution.

In the third line of Jesus' prayer (usually translated "Thy kingdom come"), the Aramaic version uses the words *teete malkutakh*. The word for "come"[10] (*teete*) suggests an urgency. It is an intensive form, something like, "Come, really come!" So other renditions of this line can be:

Let your "I Can" come through us!

Create your reign of unity now!

Desire new vision through us!

Unite our "I can" to yours!

Bring your empowerment here and now!

The following body prayer focuses on building a sense of *malkuta* in everyday life:

Breathe easily and naturally, and focus on the need for new vision in your life. Remember a time when your life demanded a definite change—in work, relationship, living situation, or anything else—and you made a change. What inner resources did you bring to bear to make those changes? Breathe with that sense of empowerment as you feel inwardly the sound of the words "tey-tey mal-ku-takh." If you cannot find the "I can" in yourself, breathe with the feeling of your need for it. Then affirm that you are opening to the possibility that malkuta *can infuse your life from all around you, from the sacred "I Can." Thereafter, whenever you recognize this quality in other people, affirm and praise it inwardly.*

This sense of self-confidence need not be egotistical. Only one "I" really exists. Sometimes we need to enlarge the sense of our personal "I" in order to allow the Universe to express its unique purpose through us. Jesus' teaching on *malkuta* presents several other basic hints to cultivate it.

SIMPLICITY COUNTS

When we take another look at the first of the Beatitudes (which we examined in chapter three), we can remember how important simplicity is to the process of inner empowerment and *malkuta*. Before we can get an agreement in our subconscious community, we need to return to the breath and realize it as our only possession. Matthew's version of the Beatitudes does not mention *malkuta* again until the eighth of these sayings, which is usually translated (KJV): "Blessed are they which are persecuted for righteousness' sake: for theirs is the kingdom of heaven" (Matthew 5:10).

It is helpful to know that the Aramaic word for "persecute"[11] can also mean to dominate, drive away, banish, or dislocate because of shame. The Aramaic word *khenuta* is translated here as "righteousness."

More literally, it means the base of justice on which something can rest. It also carries the sense of bringing all parties or voices together to be heard and considered equally. This type of justice-making occurs both inside and outside—in one's psyche and in one's community. So other translations of this Beatitude could be:

Blessedly ripe are those who are banished for seeking justice, within and without; their new home is a larger universe of empowerment.

In tune with the cosmos are those who are dominated and driven away because they long for a firm foundation of community; their domain becomes the activity that rules the cosmos.

Happy and right on time are those who draw shame for their pursuit of peace between all the conflicting voices; they realize their part in the vision that vibrates through all of creation.

We can look at the first and eighth Beatitudes together, as two parts of the same process. In the first Beatitude, we start with simplicity—the realization that breath is our only possession—and end in empowerment, *malkuta*. In the eighth Beatitude, the sense of *malkuta* is already in action—in seeking justice and pursuing peace. These actions may lead to us being driven out of our comfortable places, either physically or emotionally. Our lives could be further simplified as we find ourselves part of a larger home or purpose.

Yeshua also points to the value of simplicity for attaining *malkuta* in his famous saying about becoming like children. In the King James version:

Verily I say unto you, Except ye be converted, and become as little children, ye shall not enter into the kingdom of heaven. Whosoever therefore shall humble himself as this little child, the same is greatest in the kingdom of heaven. (Matthew 18:3-4)

Here the word translated as "converted"[12] can also mean to change, move, give back, or restore. Its roots point to alternating movements, like opening and shutting, coming and going, or to a process that proceeds contrary to expectation. If we return to a childlike state, we can experience a door opening to an aspect of self that we may have left behind.

The root of the words translated as "children" and "child" suggests an unmarried youth, one who is still under the shelter of parents, or who is covered and veiled.

The word translated as "humble" is one that we encountered previously in chapter three, when we considered the third Beatitude. It refers to liquefaction, melting, bowing down, and softening something overly rigid. Inwardly, the word can refer to an attitude of surrender that makes way for the divine "I Can" to move through one with power.

The Aramaic word translated as "greatest" (*rab*) means literally "will be multiplied" or "will grow greatly." Its root refers to a movement (R) of creation and propagation (B). The phrase translated simply "in the kingdom" in verse four also presents more meanings in Aramaic. As we've seen, the preposition that stands for "in" (*b*) can also be translated literally as several other relationships, including by, with, or among. With this in mind, the meaning of *malkuta* can be simultaneously personal, communal, and cosmic. So some additional senses of this passage are:

> *Amen—by the earth on which I stand,*
> *if you do not reenter the door of childhood*
> *and rediscover the wholehearted trust you felt*
> *in your parents' shelter,*
> *you will not enter the reign of vision-power*
> *vibrating through the universe.*
> *Like this child,*
> *the person who softens the rigid within,*

who can freely flow and go anywhere,
will grow and multiply in power
by, with, among, and in
the reign of cosmic unity.

EMPOWERMENT GROWS WILD

Jesus used many parables, or teaching stories, to try to convey what he meant by *malkuta* to his listeners. Since this state of radical change and empowerment must come from the inside out, we are brought again to the province of the subconscious self, which the Aramaic calls *naphsha*. One can influence this part of the self best by indirect methods like stories, or wordless experiences like spiritual healing.

The Aramaic word for parable[13] is derived from the word meaning to stretch out or extend a cover over something. The telling of a parable covers a process of transformation that can go on underneath its telling. Perhaps, as the saying we saw earlier from the Gospel of Thomas (113:2) implies, the notion of queen-kingdom itself is a parable or symbol that is "spread out upon the earth" in the images presented to us by nature.

We will examine a number of parables in the second half of the book that illustrate how this process of inner transformation occurs under the auspices of Holy Wisdom, or Hokhmah. For now, we will look at a few parables that help us gain a feeling for the vision-empowerment that Jesus promoted.

The parables of the mustard seed and the yeast (Matthew 13:31, 33) both present us with a process that, once begun, works on its own as though in secret (KJV):

The kingdom of heaven is like to a grain of mustard seed, which
a man took, and sowed in his field.

The kingdom of heaven is like unto leaven, which a woman took,
and hid in three measures of meal, till the whole was leavened.

Mustard is considered a weed even today in the region of Galilee. It grows freely and spreads even without being sown. According to Assyrian Aramaic scholar George Lamsa, mustard seed is not used as an edible spice in the Middle East, because it is believed to cause insanity.[14] So why would a farmer sow it? One reason might be that it adds rich nutrients like nitrogen to the soil so that the land can be used for edible crops in succeeding seasons. Thus the mustard benefits the soil—the natural community—and only indirectly the human community. Many traditional farming methods used, and still use, this method of "green composting."

In terms of the subconscious, the image of green composting points out that often some part of our being needs to be left "fallow," seemingly unproductive. Paradoxically, this allows the wild parts of our being to grow and nourish the rest of us. The inner empowerment of *malkuta* then flourishes. The Aramaic word for "mustard seed"[15] reinforces this image: it derives from a root that describes something spreading freely, like a wildfire. In his travels and ministry, Jesus emulated the mustard. He traveled without a fixed home. He visited, ate with, and touched people individually, spreading a sense of the divine "I Can" wherever he went, like wild mustard.

Similarly, yeast works to leaven bread without human effort. Its action begins within, takes time, and requires the bread maker to know the right time to knead the dough, let it rise again, and bake it. The Aramaic word for "yeast" or "leaven"[16] suggests from its roots something within a body that is hot and glowing and spreads its heat outwards.

These images of things that work from inside out underscore a primary feature of Yeshua's teaching of *malkuta*. If he could have simply said either "let's have a revolution" or "go take care of your inner life," he would not have needed to be so ambiguous. He used parables to work on the subconscious minds of his listeners in order to create an "aha!" that leads to both inner and outer change.[17]

PLANTING A SEED

As we conclude this chapter, take another moment to breathe with the sense of your deepest inner spaces. Feel your way into the wilderness of your being and look around. What do you see or sense? If nothing comes, use your active imagination to create a picture of your subconscious as a landscape. What would it look like and how would it feel if you could sense a constant presence of revivifying nature within you? As you open to the images and feelings that come, use the word mal-koo-tah *to focus your breathing. Affirm that you already have the capability to restore your inner life. In fact the process is already taking place, and has been for some time. It has led you to this meditation, in this book, in this moment. Affirm this part of your inner being as your own "I can!"—your inner queen- or kingdom—which no one can or will be allowed to violate.*

After some minutes in this space of creative imagination, slowly open your eyes, but continue to breathe the word mal-koo-tah. *As you do so, make a gradual transition in your awareness from imagination to your actual situation in life. Hold the feeling of both as elements of your present* malkutah. *Both are equally real, equally able to change your life. Take a few moments to write or draw freely, allowing whatever words or images come to reflect your inner* malkutah.

When we have firmly established a sense of this empowerment, we will begin to feel the purpose of our lives, and the purpose of Alaha as it expresses itself through us. We will move toward becoming complete human beings, living up to our nature as *adam*—beings through whom the blood and sap of the universe flows.

Part II

New Sophia: Embracing a Wider Community

Chapter Seven

BETWEEN HEAVEN AND EARTH: HOLY WISDOM UNITING DIVERSITY

Heaven and earth,
wave and particle,
individuality and community
may cross boundaries,
go beyond themselves, and
transgress their limits:
form may pass into light
and light back to form.
But the story I'm telling you will not:
the fullest expression of
the purpose of my life,
from beginning to end,
will continue.

> —alternative reading of Matthew 24:35, Mark 13:31,
> and Luke 21:33 (KJV: "Heaven and earth shall pass away,
> but my words shall not pass away.")

THE WORDS OF JESUS ABOUND IN PARADOX. AS WE HAVE SEEN IN CHAPTER FIVE, THE SACRED IDEAL OF UNITY CAN UNITE MANY SEEMING OPPOSITES. HOW THEN DOES THE MIDDLE Eastern mystical tradition make sense of the diversity that we find around us, such as the beauty of all the variegated forms of nature? How does it reconcile the conflicting demands of community, family, and individual expression? How does it propose to unite the diversity within each person: the myriad voices, feelings, desires, and thoughts that often seem a jumble, not a unity? To answer these questions we must consider first the Middle Eastern concepts of heaven and earth, and second, the role that Holy Wisdom plays in uniting them.

As we have seen previously, the Aramaic word usually translated "heaven" (*shemaya*) comes from one of the words for light that we examined in chapter five. It indicates a sacred vibration (*shem*) that vibrates without limit through the entire manifested cosmos (*-aya*). As we saw briefly in chapter three, the word for "earth" (*ar'ah*) does not simply mean the ground or the planet Earth, but can simultaneously refer to all of nature and to any being that has individual form—from a plant to a star.

Genesis begins by proposing that the first two creations in "beginning-time" were the archetypes of individual, particular existence, called earth, and of connected, communal existence, called heaven. By contrast, many of us were raised with the entirely different views of Westernized religion: earth is something we are stuck with; the body is a necessary evil; and later we will receive a reward in a disembodied place called heaven, which has nothing to do with the imperfections of earth. These interpretations shrink a very profound Jewish concept into something unrecognizable as Middle Eastern cosmology.

From an "earth" point of view, we are an array of infinitely diverse and unique beings. From a "heaven" point of view, we are connected with every being in the universe through one wave of light or sound. To look at existence from only one viewpoint is incomplete, like walking around with only one eye open. With both eyes open, we can see the depth of two realities that interpenetrate simultaneously.

CROSSING BOUNDARIES

The ancient archetypes of heaven and earth appear in the saying of Jesus translated at the beginning of this chapter. The Aramaic word for "pass away"[1] can also mean to cross over a boundary or go beyond a limit. As we saw in chapter two, the Aramaic word for "word" can mean a story or narration, the flow of anything that is fully formed, or the full expression of a life. Since heaven and earth interpenetrate, when individual forms pass away their breath and vibration enter *shemaya*. From the vibrating cosmos new forms arise. The full expression of any particular life influences the texture of the whole of reality, because every vibration, from a "heaven" perspective, is connected to every other. As a Sufi saying goes, each person has a unique note in the universal symphony; no one else can strike yours except you.[2]

That heaven can influence earth is taken for granted in most ancient traditions. A more mysterious matter addressed by the Middle Eastern mystical traditions concerns the way earth can influence heaven. I believe that Yeshua comments on this in a saying recorded in the Gospel of Thomas:

> If the flesh has come into being because of the breath, it is a marvel; but if the breath has come into existence because of the body, it is a marvel of marvels. Yet I marvel at how this great wealth has made its home in this poverty. (Saying 29)

To realize that we vibrated into form, that a sense of divine guidance influences our lives, is indeed a marvel. To consider the other side of the equation, that our individual lives may affect the whole stream of existence, boggles the mind. We can also contemplate the way in which the movement that began the cosmos—from the Big Bang onwards—still vibrates through our cells and bodies. Indeed, something mysteriously rich has taken up residence in very limited circumstances.

THE DISAPPEARING LAW

Heaven and earth passing away is mentioned again in Matthew 5:18 (KJV):

> For verily I say unto you, Till heaven and earth pass, one jot or one tittle shall in no wise pass from the law, till all be fulfilled.

The word translated here as "pass" is the same translated as "pass away" in the passage quoted at the opening of this chapter. The word for "law"[3] in Aramaic points by its roots to anything of beauty that helps relieve or take away that which deprives a human being of strength.

The worlds of heaven and earth mingle and cross their boundaries continually. But the purpose that formed the basic precepts of moral behavior for humanity will continue, as long as humanity itself is poised between earth and heaven, with the challenges that these two worlds present. Another reading of this saying from the Aramaic can be:

> Until light and form,
> individuality and community,
> heaven and earth
> finally merge again into Unity,
> not the smallest part of every
> guidance that relieves our weakness
> will pass away,
> until it has fulfilled its purpose
> and is no longer needed.

As we have seen in the last chapter, Yeshua most often uses the words "queendom" (*malkuta*) and "heaven" (*shemaya*) together. The reign of empowerment begins in the vibratory world—vision precedes form—just as it did in the Jewish creation story. Since in the realm of vibration all things are already connected, when one wishes to shift the shape of reality, one works first with the tools with which "heaven" operates: sound, atmosphere, vibration, word, light. Yeshua used exactly these tools in both his teaching and healing ministries, according to the Gospels.

Heaven and earth meet in the expression Yeshua used in the fourth line of his prayer, usually translated "Thy will be done in earth, as it is in heaven" (Matthew 6:10). The Aramaic word translated as "will"[4] can also mean desire, delight, or consent. It expresses an inner harmony of feeling that leads, of its own accord, to manifestation. When *malkuta*, the empowering vision in tune with Unity, has entered our lives, then what we normally call "will" really becomes delight. This delight is a natural expression of both our pleasure and that of the cosmos. Other readings of this line, from the Aramaic, can be:

> *Let your delight flow through us,*
> *in wave and particle.*

> *Let your pleasure manifest in us,*
> *in light and form.*

> *Let your desire act through us*
> *as communal and individual purpose.*

WHAT HEAVEN AND EARTH CAN HOLD

The native Middle Eastern view of the interplay of heaven and earth also influences another statement by Jesus in Matthew (KJV):

> *Verily I say unto you, Whatsoever ye shall bind on earth shall*
> *be bound in heaven: and whatsoever ye shall loose on earth*
> *shall be loosed in heaven.* (Matthew 18:18-19)

This passage has often been interpreted to mean that Jesus gave his followers a special ability to forgive sins. However, the Aramaic text presents another picture. The word "bind"[5] in Aramaic can mean to tie oneself to something, as well as to engage or enmesh oneself in some aspect of material existence. It can mean to harness one's energies or, symbolically, to enclose fire in a circle. The Aramaic word for "loose" is related by root and sound to the same. It presents the symbolic image of a circle opening up, of liberation, or of the umbilical cord being severed after birth.

Given that there are two worlds that interpenetrate, we then have a choice about how to use our energies: some of them invested in the world of vision and vibration, some in the world of form and manifestation. For instance, we can invest time and energy to envision a new vocation, or to change the conditions of the one we have. The image of spaciousness returns here. If we want something new to happen, we have to be willing to let go, to some extent, of what has already manifested in order to allow the possibility for what could be. If we want to preserve what we have, we need to invest energy in caring for and nurturing it. As Yeshua says elsewhere: "Where your treasure is, your heart, courage, and passion will be also" (Matthew 6:21). So a more open reading of the above passage can be:

> *What you hold onto in form*
> *will also be fixed in vision.*
> *The energy you contain in*
> *an individual effect or possession*
> *will also be bound in*
> *the field of vibrating cause.*
>
> *What you release from form*
> *will be available for vision.*
> *The energy you allow to grow*
> *beyond your own creation,*
> *cutting the cord that keeps*
> *you and it dependent,*

will liberate both into the larger
cosmos of unlimited creation.

Generally, Western psychology views those who spend too much time in the visionary or "heaven" world as more in need of help than those who invest too much time creating and protecting possessions in the "earth" one. On the other hand, the problem of being overly caught up in material existence has also been recognized as the cause of various stress disorders.

The Hebrew-Aramaic mind may have clarified this dilemma but it has not solved it. The question still remains: how do we achieve a balance? Of all the possible experiences that we could have, which do we choose? Of all of the possible occupations at which we could spend our time, which really expresses our life's work and purpose? Of all of the relationships that we could pursue, in which do we decide to invest our whole selves? Of all of the potentials, voices, and feelings within us, which do we choose to express as the "I am" of this moment? In the view of Middle Eastern mysticism, these are questions that concern the balancing of heaven and earth.

THE CROSS OF HEAVEN AND EARTH

As a body prayer, we can use a visualization to help us reaffirm the presence of both heaven and earth, *shemaya* and *ar'ah*, at any moment.

Sit or stand comfortably for a few moments. Begin to breathe,
feeling a connection through your whole body from underneath
to above. Imagine that this straight line of breath supports you
from underneath as well as pulls you from above. Imagine this
straight line to be the line of your life's story, from past to future.
Or imagine it as your connection to Alaha, an expression of your

unique purpose in life. Affirm this straight line of your life as something that is whole and complete for now and will also continue to unfold.

Then breathe a few more breaths while you bring your hands and arms slowly together in front of you to form a circle. Breathe with the circle of your existence: those with whom you feel connected as friends, family members, or coworkers. Allow the feeling of the circle to expand to include a connection with the whole human family and with all of nature. Allow the circle to become as wide as you can. Imagine it as your connection to all that vibrates, as well as to the limitless reservoir of vision and power that surrounds you.

Finally, breathe for some moments with the feeling of the two worlds interpenetrating each other, in this moment. Identify with a sense of "I" that allows you to hold both, the individual and the cosmic.

SOPHIA'S INVITATION

According to Middle Eastern mysticism, we have additional help to build a sense of self large enough to make meaning of all the diversity in life. This help comes from a figure related to another version of the Jewish creation story: Hokhmah, otherwise known as Holy Wisdom, or by her later Greek name, Sophia.

The connection between Jesus and Sophia has been noted by a number of Biblical scholars.[6] First, the sayings of Hokhmah in the book of Proverbs express the same sort of paradoxical wisdom that the sayings of Jesus do. Second, Proverbs tells a story in which Hokhmah sends out servants to gather people together to eat and drink with her, and partake of her wisdom (Proverbs 9). Jesus tells a similar story in which a rich man invites various of his friends to a dinner.[7] All are too busy to attend and give various excuses. At this point the rich man instructs his servants to go out into the streets and invite "the poor, the crippled, the blind and the lame." Finally, since room still exists, he tells his servant to invite anyone whom he comes across.

Some have interpreted this parable to mean that Jesus intended to start a church based on Gentile converts, since "the Jews" rejected him. Despite the fact that most early Christians were Jews, by any definition, this interpretation has contributed to Christian anti-Semitism. More to the point, Jesus actually emulated Hokhmah when he gathered people of many diverse backgrounds together to eat and drink with him, even when this violated the class norms of his time.

Jesus' sayings in Aramaic show another level of connection with Hokhmah, one that can illuminate the question of balancing individuality and community in one's life.

In the Beginning Was Wisdom

At this point, we need to return to the version of the Jewish creation story in Proverbs. According to this account, Hokhmah, Holy Wisdom, was also part of the creative process. For instance, in clear references to the same "beginning," "depths," and "waters" recorded in the first two verses of Genesis, Proverbs 8:22-24 reports (KJV):

The Lord possessed me in the beginning of his way, before his works of old. I was set up from everlasting, from the beginning, or ever the earth was. When there were no depths, I was brought forth; when there were no fountains abounding with water.

No doubt, Holy Wisdom is an important feminine archetype, one that has been largely neglected through much of the history of Christianity. But she is more than that. The question remains but is seldom asked: "What role did she play in creation?" I believe that part of the answer lies in her Hebrew name itself: *Hokhmah*. By a mystical reading, the roots of this word point to a breath of individuality (HO) which arises from a sense of inner-ness (KhM) and then expands to connect with Sacred Unity (A).

The roots of Hokhmah's name, as well as the way she is depicted in Proverbs, show that her role in creation was to form the first integrated self, or "I am." For instance, in the first verse quoted above, the word "possessed"[8] in Hebrew points to a centralizing force that can create a home or center of awareness. Using other expansions of the Hebrew words, I have opened up the translation of verse 22 this way:

> *As the first archetype of ordering existence,*
> *this Universal Life Force absorbed me,*
> *Hokhmah, Sacred Wisdom,*
> *Breath from Within and Underneath,*
> *into itself.*
>
> *Cosmic appetite combined with density,*
> *the desire to compress and condense,*
> *and the first "I"—the first individual experience—*
> *joined the journey from the very start.*
>
> *This was the original, most ancient mystery:*
> *how can the power of growth can be contained*
> *and fixed around a center,*
> *the identity of the self?*
> *This is the axis on which the universe turns.*[9]

Upon further reflection: We could have had a universe in which individuality was not a primary feature. It all could have been one un-differentiated whole. Or even, given a certain amount of diversity, there need not have been much individuality. We seem to see less individuality in the way flocks of birds or herds of animals travel together. Part of this flock or herd behavior is still part of our make-up, but for better or for worse, a more complex sense of "I am" became the heritage of human beings. According to this reading, it was Hokhmah's doing.

We can also hear the story of Hokhmah's invitation to eat and drink in Proverbs 9 as the way she gathers diverse parts of the self into a whole. Proverbs uses mythological language to begin this chapter: "Wisdom hath builded her house, she hath hewn out her seven pillars." The Hebrew words can also reveal other levels of meaning. For instance, "building" and "hewing" can also indicate "dividing the darkness," and "pushing from outside in." We can see these as ways that Hokhmah works as she brings separate "selves" together to unite and form an "I am."

Another example of Hokhmah uniting separate selves appears in a text from the Nag Hammadi Library, usually titled "Thunder, Perfect Mind." According to a number of scholars, the voice of this text is that of Hokhmah.[10] In a large part of it, the voice of an "I" expresses many paradoxical identities simultaneously:[11]

> I am first and last,
> honored and dishonored,
> prostitute and saint,
> experienced and virginal.

Most tellingly, another section reads:

> I am the "within."
> I am the "within" of all natures.
> In the beginning, all spirits claim my creation.
> In the end, all souls request my presence.

In still another section she says:

> You cannot fail to "know" me, anywhere or anytime.

I am both what knows and what denies knowledge.

Be aware, this moment—

don't claim ignorance of this mind. . . .

I am the silence not grasped by the mind,

the image you can't forget.

I am the voice of every natural sound,

the word that always reappears.

I am the intonation of my name.

Like the Gospel of Thomas and the rest of the Nag Hammadi Library, we have only a Coptic copy of this text. If we assume a Hebrew original, however, the last line could be seen as a play on words. The intonation of the name—*Ho-khm-ah*—expresses in sound the archetypal energies that formed the first "I am." Another literal translation of the word *Hokhmah* could be "Sacred Sense." In the same way that Sacred Breath expresses the unity of all breathing, Hokhmah embodies the coming together of all senses and sense impressions to form a self or "I." Like the sound of thunder, which unites all of one's senses in an awareness of the moment, this Sacred Sense collects and galvanizes all senses, every instant.

Modern Western psychology still does not understand these phenomena well. We are bombarded every moment with numerous sense impressions. Something within us integrates them all and allows us to say, "*I* hear, *I* smell, *I* touch, *I* taste." We know that this integration occurs because we also know of individuals in our society who have lost this ability.

While Western psychology may name this condition multiple personality disorder, schizophrenia, or something else, it has not solved the questions of either cause or treatment.[12] Often a person who has lost a healthy sense of "I am" seems to not have received healthy, loving touch in childhood, or to have received outright physical and/or emotional abuse. From a Middle Eastern standpoint, one could say that

Hokhmah was not present in the form of a parent who offered the sense of protection, love, and "invitation to the table" that would have allowed the many impressions and voices of the self to form a healthy "I."

Hokhmah unites opposites—the visionary and the embodied, the waves of sense impressions and the particular perception of an individual self. In this, she stands between, and unites, heaven and earth.

Yeshua and Hokhmah

Returning to Yeshua's emulation of Hokhmah, we can see that his insistence that the queen-kingdom was coming "from inside out," mirrors Hokhmah's work as the "within of all natures." When Yeshua uses parables, stories, and short sayings, he also emulates Hokhmah's way of working from within, through means that unite the intuitive and logical dimensions of the mind. We shall see how this works in more detail in the following chapters. Yeshua's healing ministry also emulated the ability of Hokhmah to give life and strength to those whom she calls together.[13]

When he shared meals with those considered the "untouchables" of his time, he acted out Hokhmah's creation of a new, integrated "I am" from many previously separate voices. The collective expression of this new "I am" was the new queen-kingdom—the reign of universal empowerment in the community. Yeshua criticized those in religious authority for not following the example of open-hearted invitation and justice offered by Hokhmah, and he radically reinterpreted each person's responsibility to follow in her mythic footsteps. This combination of spiritual and social teaching placed him in a dangerous position regarding both the religious and secular powers of his time.

Related to both "food" and "Hokhmah," the Aramaic word for "bread" (lakhma)[14] appears in several of Yeshua's sayings. The word is based on the same main root (KhM), and as part of the same root family can also mean understanding, or more broadly, that which feeds the "I," whether physically, emotionally, mentally, or on any other level. This word appears in the fifth line of the prayer Jesus gave, usually translated, "Give us this day our daily bread." With the Aramaic nuances added, the prayer asks not only for physical bread but for whatever nourishes a healthy sense of "I am," which can include mental, emotional or spiritual food.

Yeshua's "I am" sayings in John present another layer of meaning in light of this interpretation of Hokhmah. These statements can point to the gifts that direct contact with the "I am" within offers. Direct contact with Sacred Sense leads to an experience of simple presence, a sacred awareness of the here and now. We no longer identify with what we perceive, feel, or own, but rather with that which offers the notion of "I" to it all. As one expression of this sacred Simple Presence, we looked at the saying "I am the way, the truth, and the life" in chapter four. Yeshua expressed other examples of the gifts of Hokhmah's "I am" this way. From an Aramaic reading:

> *The "I am" leads us to the right experiences at the right time and place.*
> (KJV: "I am the good shepherd" John 10:11.)

> *Simple Presence is the food of understanding, giving life to all.*
> (KJV: "I am the bread of life" John 6:35.)

> *The "I am" gives knowledge of all levels of sensation and existence.*
> (KJV: "I am the light of the world" John 8:12.)

> *Simple presence is the door between all worlds.*
> (KJV translation: "I am the door" John 10:9.)

Once again, these statements need not refer exclusively to the person of Jesus. For them to do so, would be very un-Middle Eastern. If

Yeshua made these statements, there are many possible layers of wisdom to them in an Aramaic sense. They may indeed point to a very profound spiritual practice.

A Meditation on the "I Am"

Return to the feeling of your breathing and revisit the place inside where both the straight line and the circle of your life can meet. Where do you feel this in your body? What images arise? At the beginning, there may be simply a confusing swirl of sensation and feeling. Use the word Hokh-mah *to center your breathing. Then focus your concentration on the image of a table at which all of the various aspects of your life can come together. These might include your personal goals, your relationships, your individual purpose and its connection to the purpose that vibrate through the cosmos. At this table there is enough to fill all the mouths, and each is welcomed equally, no matter what gift they bring: the honored and the dishonored, the child and the adult. For now it is enough to affirm that such a place is possible, and that a being like Sacred Sense can actually support the birth of a new self in one's life.*

In the next chapter we will go deeper into the self and discover the different faces of the soul presented in Yeshua's Aramaic words.

Chapter Eight

SOUL, SELF, AND LIFE: THE PROVINCE OF INNER WORK

For how does it help a human being
to know diversity and abundance outside
but lack an inner life?

—alternate reading of Matthew 16:26, Mark 8:36, and Luke 9:25
(KJV: "For what is a man profited, if he shall gain
the whole world and lose his own soul?")

IN CHAPTER SIX ON QUEENDOM, I MENTIONED THE SEMITIC NO-
TION OF THE SUBCONSCIOUS SELF, CALLED *NAPHSHA* IN ARAMAIC
AND *NEPHESH* IN HEBREW. IN FACT, THESE TERMS POINT TO A
range of ideas and images having to do with different faces of what we
usually call the soul or the individual self. There is no adequate one-
word translation of the Aramaic word *naphsha*, so in this chapter I have
often left the word untranslated as one might use the word *tao* in a
discussion of Chinese spirituality.

If we begin by looking at the various images of the self or soul that
Middle Eastern psychology presents, we can then consider the way
the word *naphsha* is used in the sayings of Jesus. This subject has
been made more confusing than necessary by the fact that the usual
New Testament translations do not translate the word *naphsha* (or its
Greek equivalent) consistently. In one case, we find it translated "soul,"
in another "self," and in still another "life." All told, *naphsha* is used
more than two hundred times in the Gospels. As we begin to unravel

its meaning and usage, various sayings of Yeshua will become clearer and more useful for our own inner work.

In an ancient Semitic sense, one does not "have" or "possess" a soul: one *is* a soul. Further, like the meditation on the candle flame we used earlier, the soul has different aspects. Like breath-spirit, the soul-self is really a continuum that connects the "heavenly" or vibrational aspect of being with the "earthly" or particular aspect.

The *naphsha* represents the aspect of soul-self that usually feels itself more on the "earth" side of the continuum. For most of us, our sense of spiritual guidance feels separate from our subconscious self, where many emotional dramas and traumas get played out. Just as Sacred Breath connects our personal breath to cosmic spirit, Sacred Sense or Hokhmah links our individual sense of "I" to the "I Am." In this view, the journey of life asks us to fully realize our connections with Unity. We do not so much purge or empty our *naphsha* of all of its problematic elements as allow each element to find its place at the table of Hokhmah and Alaha.

To speak in this way takes us into mythic or poetic language. The reality of the layers of the soul and its deepest mysteries transcends any human language. We use words and images to try to make sense of them, in order to help all aspects of our self assimilate what must remain a wordless experience of realization.

The aspects of our *naphsha* that seem problematic to us are best approached by indirect means, akin to the swirling, seemingly chaotic, intuitive energy we found at the beginning of Genesis. Parables and stories do this best. But before we approach them, let's examine some of the sayings of Yeshua about the *naphsha* aspect of the soul-self.

LOVING THE *NAPHSHA*

In an interaction reported in Matthew and Mark, someone confronted Jesus with a question: Which is the greatest or most important commandment in the law? He answered by quoting the Jewish scriptures (KJV):[1]

> *Thou shalt love the Lord thy God with all thy heart, and with all thy soul, and with all thy mind, and with all thy strength: this is the first commandment. And the second is like, namely this, Thou shalt love thy neighbour as thyself.* (Mark 12:30-31)

In the first commandment, the word translated "soul" is *naphsha* in Aramaic. In the second, the word "thy-*self*" is the same word. So in both cases, he points toward a process that includes what we would call the subconscious self, just like the Jewish scripture he quotes.[2] The Greek New Testament uses the word *psuche* for "soul" here. It is the origin of our word *psyche*, which also has clear relations to what we would call the inner or psychic life.

The Aramaic word translated here as "love" is *rehem*,[3] meaning a love or compassion that can pour from the depths of oneself, from an inner "womb," the province of Hokhmah. The Aramaic word usually translated as "lord" (*mare*) is difficult to translate. The word's roots suggest obvious power and majesty; it is the aspect of the sacred that catches our attention without any resort to reasoning or logic.

The Aramaic word for "heart," *leba*, refers not simply to the physical heart, but figuratively to the center of one's feeling or intelligence, the pith or marrow of what we would call our mental-emotional life.

The word "mind" in Aramaic is related by root to a verb meaning to herd or feed. This aspect of the mind follows blindly and grasps things in an instinctual sense. In Western scientific terms we might compare this with the older, "animal" layer of the brain or intelligence.[4]

The word translated as "strength" (*hayye*) is the same we have seen previously as "life," meaning life force or energy. Given these extra pieces of the puzzle, we can see that both the Jewish commandment and the

way Jesus renders it in Aramaic point to a process that involves all parts
of the soul:

> *Let compassion unfurl from your inner womb*
> *for Sacred Unity*
> *in the form that impresses you most deeply,*
> *inside or out.*
> *Send this love with and through*
> *your whole passionate self,*
> *your whole awakening, subconscious self,*
> *your whole instinctive mind,*
> *and with all of your life energy.*

When we engage our whole self in this type of deep love-compas-
sion, it can integrate our whole personality, as can the power of devotion that we explored in the chapter on holiness. The act of loving clari-
fies and brings together many separate parts of our being.

The second commandment asks us to extend this same deep love
toward our neighbor. In Aramaic, the word for "neighbor"[5] indicates
anyone who draws near to us, or somehow appears in close proximity.
Neighbors cannot be identified as friends, enemies, or family; they are
simply there. Because Aramaic frequently blurs the distinction between
inside and outside, we can also think of a neighbor as a member of our
inner community. So other layers of the second commandment are:

> *Give birth to love for the one "next door,"*
> *as you do for your own soul-self*
> *and the part of it that feels like a neighbor.*

> *Give birth to compassion for the nearest,*
> *yet unfamiliar, aspect of your self,*
> *as you do for the one outside*
> *who feels like a stranger.*

Give birth to the deepest warmth for
the neighbor, inside and out,
as you do for your own
subconscious community,
inside and out.

A MEDITATION ON THE INNER NEIGHBOR

Allow yourself a brief moment to breathe easily and naturally into the deepest place inside you. Bring into your focused awareness all of the love that you can breathe in at this moment, using the spark of whatever feels most sacred to you in your life. This need not be something religious. It can be whatever has created a sense of illuminating space in your life. With this feeling riding on your breath, place your hands lightly over your heart for a few moments and open to this love. Then move your hands and the feeling of your breathing, to your belly. Offer the same unconditional love to your naphsha, the awakening community of self within. Then after some moments, move your hands gently to your head and offer this support to your whole nervous system and to your instinctive self, the part of you that maintains the body.

Then relax your hands and arms, and breathe in and out as much life energy as you can at this moment, combined with compassionate love. Finally, reopen a channel to your naphsha and offer this sense of unconditional life and love to all the parts of your being that feel separate or unfamiliar. Don't force this blessing, but simply offer it with respect and without any expectation to the "nearest stranger" within you. As you complete the meditation, lengthen the feeling of your breathing to include those in

your outer life and outer community: friends, family, neighbors,
and all beings. Give thanks for all of these faces of diversity in
your life.

LOSING THE *NAPHSHA*

For a further understanding of the *naphsha*, we can look at a well-known statement Jesus made about losing the soul, part of which I have retranslated to open this chapter. Here is the longer passage in Mark, as translated in the King James version:[6]

> *For whosoever will save his life shall lose it; but whosoever shall*
> *lose his life for my sake and the gospel's, the same shall save it.*
> *For what shall it profit a man, if he shall gain the whole world,*
> *and lose his own soul?* (Mark 8:35-36)

In the first verse, the Aramaic word for "lose"[7] can also mean to go astray, be destroyed, or fall into decay. Its roots suggest a process of self-surrender: something has grown to the furthest extent of its development and then bows itself in service to what is greater.

The word for "save" in Aramaic (*heyya*) comes from *hayye*, the word we saw in the passage above meaning strength or life force. In this sense, saving the *naphsha* means giving it life energy. Paradoxically, one must give the *naphsha* energy for it to develop, but its natural development should lead it to surrender its sense of separateness when it makes a full connection with *ruha*, or breath-spirit. The small self seems to be extinguished, yet it still continues in a transformed way as part of a greater "I Am."

The word for "gospel"[8] in Aramaic derives from a word that can mean to hope, consider, or endure. The expression of these qualities could be called the real "good news." From its roots this word points to the containment of a sacred fire, which instead of burning out of control provides warmth and heat over a period of time.

In the second verse, the word for "gain"[9] can also mean to surpass, exceed, or have an abundance of something. The word for "lose"—a different one than in the previous verse—can also mean to lack, be in want of, or be incomplete. So this passage could also be read:

> *Everyone who desires to give energy*
> *to his separate, subconscious self*
> *will eventually find that self surrendered,*
> *extinguished in the Only Self.*
> *Everyone who surrenders her separate self,*
> *the way I have done and hoped for,*
> *will give energy to it.*
> *For what advantage do you have if*
> *your development in form exceeds*
> *all that the world can offer,*
> *but your soul remains incomplete?*

LIFE AND MORE LIFE

As we have seen in passages like "I am the bread of life," there are many instances where the word "life" that appears in the usual translations is not *naphsha*, but rather *hayye*—life energy or life force. These include passages like John 10:10 (KJV):

> *I am come that they might have life,*
> *and that they might have it more abundantly.*

The Greek text uses the word *zoee* here, which also carries a sense of aliveness or physical energy. However, the general tendency has been to translate such words into English in a way that obscures their embodied character. This again stems from the Western concept of a split between heaven and earth. Certainly it changes the sense of the passage to translate it as:

> I have come that they might have energy
> and that they might have it in abundance
> (or: that they might have all the abundance that goes with it).

This would certainly provide a touchstone for one's participation in any spiritual or religious ritual in Jesus' name. Does it provide the life energy that he promised?

In the Aramaic version *hayye* also appears in passages that mention "eternal life," which occur most often in John. Here again, the tendency is to assume that such eternal life must be later, somewhere other than here and now. The word for "eternity" in Aramaic is *'alma*,[10] the same word translated as "world" in Mark 8:36, at the opening of the chapter. This word can also mean age, generation, or era. It is based on a root that means youth or newness, that is, everything that constantly arises new, in diversity, and in the worlds of form.[11]

With these perspectives we can also reconsider an often-quoted passage, John 3:16 (KJV):

> For God so loved the world, that he gave his only begotten Son,
> that whosoever believeth in him should not perish, but have everlasting life.

The word for "begotten,"[12] can also mean single, solitary, or united in all aspects of being. The word for "believe" (*etamen*) is based on the same root as *amen*, and suggests a sense of confidence, trust, or firmness coming from a rooted place. We saw Yeshua use another form of this word, translated as "faith"(*haimanuta*) in chapter two when we examined his healing ministry. The word for "perish" is the same word as "lose" in Mark 8:35—to decay, fade away, or lose.

So another hearing, based on the Aramaic text, can be:

For Unity so loved Diversity,
all the worlds of form,
that it brought you a child of Unity,
fulfilled in all aspects of self,
so that whoever would have
the same confidence in their own fulfillment,
like the earth underneath supporting all,
would not fade with their form,
but continue, from world to world,
with and in the ever-living Life.

THE SOUL PLAYING HIDE AND SEEK

The *naphsha* may seem to behave as a separate being, but in a worldview where Sacred Unity includes all, no being is ever totally separate. We may feel some aspects of our self to be difficult, perhaps those associated with our past. Most often we find these hiding or in exile. We may feel proud of other aspects of ourselves, perhaps those associated with where we want to go. These may reveal themselves clearly, or they may be hidden as well. In the Semitic view of the soul, these voices are like a community or committee that attempts to come to agreement. The degree of cooperation can be heard in the amount of confidence expressed in our voices at any moment.

Teaching stories and parables use their own "hide-and-seek" style to address hidden parts of the soul. Because a Middle Eastern teaching story can both reveal and hide meaning, various Sufi orders use them for "unlearning." The stories are not intended to communicate a truth, but rather, using paradox or humor, to erase a preconception from the mind of the listener that stands in the way of change. The ability of a story or parable to do this lies at the heart of another seemingly puzzling statement of Yeshua quoted by Mark (KJV):

> *Unto you it is given to know the mystery of the kingdom of God:*
> *but unto them that are without, all these things are done in parables:*
> *That seeing they may see, and not perceive; and hearing they may*
> *hear, and not understand; lest at any time they should be con-*
> *verted, and their sins should be forgiven them.* (Mark 4:11-12)

On the face of it, Jesus seems to be a bit perverse here. If he wants a wholesale change of heart on the part of his listeners, why hide things? Again, based on the Greek version, this passage has been interpreted to mean that Jesus intended to set up a select (perhaps predestined) elite, while others were doomed to failure and damnation from the start. When we look at the Aramaic text, however, another picture emerges.

The word for "know"[13] here is directly related to the Hebrew-Aramaic word for hand as well as to the word for power (the hand gives power to manipulate). This type of knowing gives one the ability to handle something.

What is handled by a parable is "mystery" (in Aramaic, *raza*), which can refer to any secret as well as to a mystical signification, symbol, or sign. The roots of this word convey the idea of the extreme thinness or even disappearance of something material, as well as of an inner movement or sound. Jesus refers to an inner process here, one which has to do with the sense of the ego seeming to disappear as an entirely new image of the self is born.

The expression "them that are without" appears in the Aramaic text as *l'baraya*,[14] which derives from the word for open countryside, or a wild area. Symbolically, it indicates the border or circumference of any area, or the fruit which is produced by the inner germ of a seed. The parable speaks to the wild parts of the self, or those that are on the outside looking in. We can only influence these areas of our being through indirect, poetic language, not simple, directive statements. As we saw in chapter six, the Aramaic word for "parable" points to one process that veils or protects another.

So the first part of Yeshua's statement, heard with Aramaic ears, might also sound like this:

You who understand need only
the barest suggestion
in order to transform
and find the "I can" within:
one part of you already knows what I'm saying.
Parables are a time-release remedy
for you who don't understand
and who are in the wilderness of your souls,
waiting to hear the invitation
to come home.

In the second part, the Aramaic words for "see," "hear," and "understand" all have double meanings.[15] "See" can mean physical seeing and also a vision that one might receive in an instant. The word for "hear" can also mean an inner sound or mystical vibration; it is a modified form of *shem*, one of the words for light. The word for "understand" is related to a noun that means an enclosure, cover, or an end or limit to things. Figuratively, the enclosure protects and hides something. Like a parable itself, it both hides and reveals.

The word translated "lest" or "unless"[16] can have a number of other meanings in Aramaic: except, perhaps, or "it may be." The word for "convert" here can mean return, answer, give back, or cause to turn. It is related to the word for face, front, or the first appearance of something. Unlike the word for "repent" that we considered earlier, this type of turning begins in response to something outwardly astonishing or striking.

We saw the Aramaic word for "forgive"[17] in chapter three on breath, meaning something that is restored to its original state, or allowed to return. Another word we saw in the same chapter, "sin" (*khataha*), can mean a frustrated hope, something that misses, or a wrongly sewn thread. It derives from the word meaning to dig out or to sew—both having to do with an effort (KH) made against a resistance (T).[18]

So with all of our word-threads in hand, the following multiple meanings begin to appear, which might have been heard by Yeshua's listeners (or perhaps parts of themselves):

These wild parts of you
see but aren't yet illuminated,
hear but aren't struck by the sound that
envelopes the mystery of Unity;
not until they (and you)
are turned around by parable,
not until turning you begin to release
the cords with which you
tie your selves to the past.

For the parts of the self that can hear a subtle message, change occurs; for those that take things more literally, the images remain in order to work in secret, like the mustard seed or the yeast. A story or parable gets one's attention, but also prevents one (or some part of the self) from thinking that a simple statement expresses everything. The empowerment that Yeshua teaches arises from an "I can" that transcends dualities and simple black-and-white answers to problems. For the parts of the self that want simple answers but in fact really need to unlearn some of their preconceptions, the parable works to mend what is broken or tangled, and to restore something to its original state. Such a deep healing of the psyche can occur on both within an individual and in the community.

The image of a parable working with the hidden depths of our *naphsha* also lies at the heart of a saying of Jesus in the Gospel of Thomas:

If you bring forth that which is within yourselves,
that which you possess will save you.
If you do not possess (or find) that within yourselves,
that which you do not possess will kill you. (Saying 70)

What is most hidden often becomes the greatest strength. Or the failure to give birth to it may lead to a life of frustration.

The image of wild and domesticated parts of the self, which we saw in the passage from Mark 4 above, also finds its way into Yeshua's story of the prodigal son (Luke 15:11-32). After he spends his inheritance, the "wild" son finds himself at rock bottom, sitting with the pigs. When he turns and lets go of all that he thought he was, including his pride, he is forgiven and welcomed home again. But at that point, the "good" son, the one who stayed home and took care of business, reacts angrily to his father's welcome feast for his returned brother. This mirrors what happens when an exiled part of our psyche is welcomed back: the whole inner family has to realign itself. All the inner voices need to let go of an image that binds the *naphsha* and prevents it from fully realizing its nature as divine.

OPENING THE DOOR OF RETURN

Return again to breathing gently with a sense of love and life energy with your inner community of selves. To help center the body prayer, you can breathe with the Aramaic word rahm, *deep unconditional love, or* hayye, *life energy. Imagine your inner psyche as a beautiful clearing in nature where all aspects of the self can gather. Imagine that all the paths to this clearing provide free and unobstructed access to the deepest parts of yourself. When each aspect is ready to be transformed, it will arrive in its*

own time, awaited by an atmosphere of love and respect. Prac-
tice waiting with love, but without urgency or even expectation.

After a few minutes, conclude by breathing with a feeling of
gratitude for whatever has occurred, even if it is only a moment's
peace and quiet.

Chapter Nine

THE PERFECT AND THE GOOD: COMPLETENESS AND TIMING

Be complete:
develop yourself to the fullest degree,
just as the Source of All
constantly bears fruit,
completing all movements
in Unity.

> —a reading of Matthew 5:48 from the Aramaic
> (KJV: "Be ye therefore perfect, even as
> your Father which is in heaven is perfect.")

THE IMAGERY OF INVITING ALL PARTS OF OURSELVES HOME, BACK TO THE TABLE LIKE THE PRODIGAL SON, LIES AT THE HEART OF THE ARAMAIC SENSE OF WHAT IT MEANS TO BE perfect. In the passage above, the word for "perfect" (*gmar*)[1] comes from a verb meaning to accomplish, fulfill oneself, or be complete. A secondary meaning is to be completely consumed, cease, or disappear. The Aramaic picture of the soul links these seeming opposites. When self-images held by the *naphsha* are no longer needed, when they have fulfilled their purpose, they fade away and are transformed as though in a rebirth. The Greek Gospel text uses the word *teleios* here, which carries a similar meaning of being mature or complete. Unfortunately,

129

both the Aramaic and Greek meanings of "perfect" have been generally ignored in favor of an interpretation of this passage implying that a state of doctrinal purity or right belief makes one perfect.

The word for "father" (*abba*)[2] can also mean parent, ancestor, or founder. It is based on the root AB, which points to all movements that seek to complete themselves or find an end. The root also refers to the desire to have, as well as to that which bears fruit. As we shall see in the next chapter, this root also helps form the root of one of the words for love in Hebrew and Aramaic. *Abba* appears in various forms in the Aramaic Gospels. As the form *abwoon*, which is used in the Lord's Prayer, it can refer to parenting in the cosmic sense, which is beyond gender. From a close reading of its individual letter-roots, this form indicates a process or a being that begins in Unity (A) and gives birth (B) via breath (U) to new forms (N).

Another, more expanded interpretation of the above passage from Matthew could be:

> *Be fulfilled in all of your selves,*
> *know them until they cease to know themselves,*
> *grow with them until they outgrow themselves*
> *in a reborn "I am."*
> *The Knowing, Growing, Parenting*
> *of the cosmos*
> *completes itself through you.*

A saying in the Gospel of Thomas advocates the same idea of completeness:

> *When you come to know yourselves, then you will be known and you will realize that you are the children of the living Father. But if you do not come to know yourselves, then you exist in poverty and you are poverty.* (Saying 3:4)

WAITING FOR COMPLETENESS

If we accept this completeness as a goal for our life's work, the questions arise: How and when do we get there? What do we do with our incompleteness in the meantime? To answer these questions, we need to consider the Aramaic sense of two words considered briefly in the introduction: "good" and "evil." These words have more non-Middle-Eastern baggage attached to them than any others we have considered so far. To begin to unload this baggage, imagine the following scene with me:

The smell of apple, almond, and sycamore trees in blossom. The sight of riotously colorful wildflowers in bloom on a hillside above the Sea of Galilee. The sound of thousands of variegated waterbirds—egrets, herons, and cranes—following their intricate and beautiful migratory patterns up the Jordan River rift valley, just at the right time. The black basalt hills above the Sea of Galilee, providing rich, dark, but very thin soil upon which to sow. The strong winds blowing in from the Mediterranean at particular times of the day.

In such a setting, timing was essential for success in planting. In Yeshua's day, the whole area of Galilee was much wetter than it is now—virtually a jungle in many areas. Water buffalo and lion roamed about. To travel safely through this wild landscape depended on knowing when certain areas were flooded, when animals that might be dangerous to humans were present, and when and where one could find edible food.[3]

Yeshua experienced all of these sensations of the natural world around him as it followed the rhythm of Sacred Unity. To describe this rhythm of rightness and ripeness, the Aramaic language uses the word *taba*,[4] usually translated "good." From its roots, the word points to something that maintains its integrity and health (T) by an inner sense of growth in harmony with what surrounds it (B).

The Gospels quote Jesus using the word *taba* in several different ways. In one sense it means that which is in tune, in time, and in harmony with Sacred Unity. Those who are "good" are at the right place and the right time with the right action. In this sense, they are prepared for any event—ready, with full presence in the moment. A derivative of this word means to prepare or make ready, as in Luke 3:4, where John the Baptist quotes Isaiah: "Prepare ye the way of the Lord." In the same sense, one can also make oneself ready for Passover.[5] As we saw previously, transforming the soul-self asks for an ever more refined sense of timing and readiness. Everything does not happen at once.

By contrast, that which is *bisha*[6] in Aramaic—usually translated "evil"—has fallen out of rhythm with Sacred Unity. This may mean that the being or act in question has been delayed in its progress and is not yet ready for the purpose for which it is meant. Or it may mean that the being or act is no longer ripe: at one time and place it was appropriate, but it has now departed from the rhythm of the sacred "I Am" and has become rotten, so to speak. On the inner level, these qualities of unripeness can apply to the images of the self held by the *naphsha* and the way that different voices within the subconscious present themselves to the conscious mind.

We can compare these concepts to those in the Greek New Testament text, which uses the word *agathos* for good—defined as being generous or kind. The word used for evil, *poneros*, comes from a verb that means to toil, so what is evil is toilsome or causes extra effort. These meanings contrast with those in Aramaic in that they emphasize different cultural values. The Greek focuses on the human-to-human relationship and on saving time, whereas the Aramaic stresses coming into rhythm or timing with nature as an expression of Unity.

Upon reflection, we only know the unripe when we compare it to the ripe. The state of harmony, or in-time-ness, lies at the heart of every being or action, no matter how veiled by disharmony it may have become. An evil that is separate from the Unity of Alaha does not exist in the Aramaic of Jesus.

GOOD AND EVIL TREES

Yeshua's saying about the ripe and unripe trees further illustrates the Aramaic concept of good and evil. The following version is from Matthew 7:15-20.[7] In order to show what the Aramaic concepts bring to the passage, I have substituted "ripe" for "good," and "unripe" for "evil" and "corrupt" in the King James version.

> *Beware of false prophets, which come to you in sheep's clothing, but inwardly they are ravening wolves. Ye shall know them by their fruits. Do men gather grapes of thorns, or figs of thistles? Even so every ripe tree bringeth forth ripe fruit; but an unripe tree bringeth forth unripe fruit. A ripe tree cannot bring forth unripe fruit, neither can a unripe tree bring forth ripe fruit. Every tree that bringeth not forth ripe fruit is hewn down, and cast into the fire. Wherefore by their fruits ye shall know them.*

A tree may go many seasons without fruit, if that is part of its natural cycle. One cannot expect an unripe tree to bear fruit out of season or out of its year. Knowing the cycle, the season, the soil, and the tree calls for a process of moment-by-moment discrimination. At a certain point, one may decide that a tree will not ripen again, in the sense that it will not bear fruit for human beings. Perhaps this particular tree, like an image held in the *naphsha*, has outlived its usefulness. It may then be time to consciously consign it to the fire and back to the earth.

We need the same type of discrimination when we consider the validity of a prophet or spiritual director. It may take time to determine what the "fruit" of a person actually is. At the time of Jesus, a number of prophets and healers made claims to be a messiah, king, or "son of David." Based on these claims, many of them fomented ill-fated rebellions against the Romans. The fruits of their efforts could be seen in the divisiveness they spread in the community at large and ultimately in the suffering they caused.

THE SOIL OF OUR SELVES

The parable of the sower and the seed further illustrates Yeshua's use of the word *taba*. This story appears in all three synoptic Gospels.[8] In this story, a person scatters seed on various types of ground. In one case the seed falls by the wayside, where birds eat it. In the second, it falls on stony ground, where there is not enough soil to support it. It has a quick spurt of first growth, but then the sun rises and scorches it, because it has "no depth of earth." In the third case, the seed falls on thorny earth, where it grows, but is eventually choked out. In the fourth case, the seed falls on "good ground" where it bears fruit.

We will take a closer look at this parable, because it has been interpreted so often as distinguishing between "believers" and "non-believers" in Jesus.

First, let us look at the commentary Yeshua himself gave. All three versions present an exasperated Yeshua giving an explanation of the parable afterwards, frustrated that his disciples don't understand the story. In Mark 4, this explanation is preceded by the passage about parables hiding and revealing things, which we considered in the previous chapter. The explanations that Yeshua gives in the three Gospels focus on different types of people who receive the "word of God" (symbolized by the seed). Many scholars feel that these explanations of the parable were added later, in order to help the early Christian church distinguish between "believers" and "non-believers." The Aramaic version offers us another view of them. If Jesus gave these explanations, then they themselves were also parables, hiding as much as they revealed.

As we saw in chapter seven on heaven and earth, the Aramaic word for "word" can refer to a flow or narration—something that proceeds from beginning to end. It has to do more with the vibrational world of *shemaya* than with the particle world of *ar'ah*. To receive the word or story of Alaha, then, focuses us on coming into right timing with Sacred

Unity. The various "people" or "soils" can also be viewed as aspects of our inner community.

Various other words in the parable itself also support this interpretation. The Aramaic word for "sow"[9] can mean to scatter or spread abroad, generate, or propagate. The related word for seed points by its roots to a layered reality in which something inside is drawn outward into manifestation by the conditions that surround it.[10] The same word can also refer to the "seed" of the self, the *naphsha*, which is the most dense face of the soul.

The Aramaic word (*nephal*) for the "fall" of the seed points by its roots to the *naphsha*, with which it shares one of its roots. The word indicates something that changes its state by scattering, if it is solid, and by distilling, if it is liquid. Figuratively, this recalls the process of exhalation and inhalation, expanding and condensing that we saw in the Genesis creation story. We can also regard the seed, the sower, and the earth as aspects of our subconscious, and the story as telling the way it embodies impressions that we receive.

The seed that falls by the wayside is eaten by birds. Jesus provides the following interpretation, as given in the usual translations (here, KJV):

> And these are they by the way side, where the word is sown; but when they have heard, Satan cometh immediately, and taketh away the word that was sown in their hearts. (Mark 4:15)

Here the key is the untranslated word *satan*, which comes from the Aramaic *satana*,[11] and simply means adversary, or that which causes one to turn aside or go astray.[12] Only later did Christian theology establish the idea of "Satan" as a being almost equal to God, and certainly not part of the divine. This notion of an "anti-God" is entirely un-Jewish.[13] In the original parable, birds carry away the seed. The Aramaic word for "bird"[14] used in this part of the story derives from a verb that means to fly about, flutter, squander, dissipate, or diffuse something. It points to a quality of mind or an aspect of the self that is reluctant to concentrate or focus.

In the section about the seed that falls on rocky ground with no depth, the Aramaic word translated as "rock"[15] is derived from the verb meaning to stop up or obstruct something. It is used metaphorically in Aramaic to mean closing the senses or heart. It also points to a head-long or ill-considered action—"hard-headed" in our way of speaking. The word for "depth" derives from another word that means to dig, hollow out, or search for something—all actions that require effort.

The sun scorches and withers the seed because it is exposed and has no root. The Aramaic word for "root" comes from a verb that, para-doxically, means to uproot or make something barren. That is, a firm root requires displacing something else: for every gain there is a loss. This points to an aspect of self that moves impulsively and does not search deeply or give up any preconceived ideas. When the "sun" (the Aramaic word for which is related to *shem*, or light) reveals this lack of depth of commitment, the new growth fades away.

In the case of the seed that is choked by thorns, the word for "thorn"[16] comes from a verb that means to feel pain or sorrow. The word's roots suggest anything that arrests one's natural growth or holds one back. Pain can spur inner growth or suffocate it. In this case, the pain is too great for the self to grow beyond it, at least for the moment.

This is not, as some have implied, a story about a sloppy farmer. Even today on the hillsides of Galilee, one finds very thin topsoil over basalt rock. These conditions make this method of sowing very practi-cal. Of all the soils that receive the seed, one will be ripe. The soil that is ready may not only be hard to find, but due to the prevailing winds, it may only be ready at certain times of the day and under certain mois-ture conditions. One could try to be very careful and only sow at certain times and places, but even so, with so many factors involved, some scattering of seed would be necessary.

In our inner selves, the same procedure can be just as effective. When we try to "micro-manage" our *naphsha*, we risk over-controlling aspects of our self that may have some reason for existence, some role in the purpose our lives that we have yet to see. A process of growth that tries to fix every problematic aspect of the self is self-defeating. Like the action of a parable, which is broadcast widely so that everyone (inner and outer) can hear what they need to hear, effective cultivation of our inner soil may sometimes mean that we simply seed a "flow of Unity" without expectation, and allow what happens to happen.

To be "good" in light of these insights is not a matter of doctrinal purity or of predestination (although both interpretations have been made). The ripe soil in our own being may change from day to day, or from moment to moment. We sow and receive repeatedly; the process does not happen once for all time. As an Aramaic reading of the seventh Beatitude puts it: "Blessedly ripe are those who plant peace, every season."

MEDITATION ON SACRED GROUND

Breathing in and out the word Alaha, *ask for the blessing of ripeness as you prepare to contact your inner self. As the Jewish teaching story goes, once you plant a seed, it is better not to dig it up repeatedly to see if it has grown. Patience and timing are required. Is this the right time to contact your* naphsha? *If you receive an inner "yes," return to a relaxed sense of breathing into your belly and imagine there sacred earth, sacred ground. You are not only the sower and the seed, but also the earth itself. What different types and textures of earth can you feel yourself to be?*

Continue to breathe Alaha *with a sense of readiness and patience. Let the flow of your breathing remind you of your place*

in the whole story of the universe as it has unfolded from the first
fireball until your present breath. Feel this flow as the word and
seed of Unity. The way that it grows through you, in the fulfill-
ment of the purpose of your life, offers your unique gift back to
the cosmos. Give thanks for the ability to give this gift.

More Stories about Unusual Farming Methods

In Matthew, after the sower and seed parable, Yeshua tells another
story about planting and timing (13:24-30). A farmer sows wheat seed
that is ready and ripe for planting. During the night, an enemy comes
along and sows similar seed—probably one of the inedible, wild varieties of wheat common in Galilee—which the King James version translates as "tares."[17] Instead of telling his servants to try to root out the
inedible sprouts, the farmer asks them to wait. They might make a mistake by rushing the process, because both varieties look very similar at
an early stage. Only at harvest is the difference plain, and that will be
the right time to separate them.

The word translated here as "enemy,"[18] which we have seen before, can also mean an owner, or a head of a family. It comes from a root
verb that means to dispute, or to inquire in a hostile manner. Figuratively, we can see it as an aspect of self that, up until now, has controlled our inner territory and provided strategies that seemed necessary for survival. When something radically new is suggested, or a new
aspect of self is revealed, it may sow seeds of distrust or argument to
dissuade us from making any change. These seeds can appear similar
to genuine new growth as they arise in our being. And yet, they also
may serve a certain purpose. The "tares" hold the soil in place. When
they have served their purpose, they can easily be gathered together
and burned to fuel the further growth of the soul.

This story implies a view of nature in which what we call weeds are acknowledged as a necessary, healthy part of the ecosystem, even where an edible crop is desired.[19]

The parable about the laborers and the vineyard (Matthew 20:1-16) presents the notion of right timing in a different light. When grapes are ripe, they must be harvested immediately, especially if they are to be used for wine. There is no tomorrow, so to speak. The owner of the vineyard hires a certain number of workers early in the morning. When he checks their progress at the third hour, he sees that they are not as fast as he had hoped. He hires more workers. He does the same at the sixth, ninth, and eleventh hours. The question arises: Which workers are more valuable? The ones who started early and worked steadily all day, or the ones who, by being available as late as the eleventh hour, made it possible to finish the job on time? The owner gives everyone the same wages, and the workers who came early complain. The owner responds (with the Aramaic nuances added):

> Don't I have the power, in harmony with Unity, to do what I want with my own? Or is your eye unripe—not satisfied with the present—because I am ripe—taking care of my own, in the right time?[20]

The story stresses being ready and available, even at the last moment, to do what is necessary. What seems like tardiness may paradoxically turn out to be a strength when it is combined with availability. From one standpoint, the actions of the vineyard owner aren't fair. But the story is not about fairness; it's about timing. The workers who came later may not have earned their wages in labor, but they did in availability. When absolutely needed, they were there. Like the seemingly unworthy guests in Yeshua's story of the invitation to a feast, they were ready when called. They were, so to speak, ripe enough.

THE FIRST AND THE LAST

Yeshua then concludes the story with a mysterious commentary on the whole notion of timing (KJV):

So the last shall be first, and the first last:
for many be called, but few chosen. (Matthew 20:16)[21]

The Aramaic word for "last"[22] comes from a verb that means to tarry, delay, linger, or remain behind. In the sense of "those who come after," it also refers to one's descendants. The word translated as "first" also means that which is before or has existed from the most ancient times. Yeshua plays with the meanings of these words. The part of the soul that is the last to be unified with Alaha may be that which is the most ancient, the innermost part of the seed, so to speak. That which wakes up first may be more superficial, not as deep, figuratively speaking. And so the realization of the most stubborn aspect of our being, or the most "primitive" part of our consciousness, may be more profound than that which came more easily, our more "modern," rational understanding.

The word translated as "many"[23] comes from a verb that means to increase, multiply, or make abundant. Its roots reveal the image of a circle opening. The word translated as "few" comes from a verb that means to diminish, become weakened by fear of the future, or be hemmed in on all sides by material existence.

The Aramaic for "called" (*q'ra*)[24] can mean to invoke or invite. It is related to the biblical Hebrew *kara*, which can also mean to engrave or hollow out. *Kara* is used in the Jewish creation story, where Elohim calls forth the potential of or "engraves" each new reality on the becoming Universe.[25] The word for "chosen" (*g'ba*) also means approved or gathered. It recalls the Hebrew *gebe*, meaning waters gathered in a pool, cistern, or lagoon. Bringing the rhyming words *q'ra* and *g'ba* together, Jesus creates the image of a space hollowed out, where waters naturally find their way to gather. This suggests the many parts of ourselves (or our communities) that join things easily: they go with the crowd when conditions are favorable. Fewer are those parts of ourselves that can persevere under difficult conditions; they flow like water between the rocks toward their destination. With nuances of the Aramaic added, the two verses can read:

> So that which remains,
> the last to arrive,
> is the most ancient of days,
> the primordial before.
> And that which comes first,
> the knowing that's easy,
> may tarry in depth
> of understanding the All.
> The many get invited:
> when life's circle opens,
> it is easy to join,
> the earth has been dug,
> and the pool is prepared.
> But the few arrive:
> hemmed in by life's troubles
> they can flow like water
> toward the gathering place.

THE SHEPHERD OF RIPENESS

As I noted briefly in chapter seven, one of the gifts of Hokhmah, Sacred Wisdom, is to lead us to the right experiences at the right moment. This can happen any time we contact the "I am" within us. As Yeshua said, "Simple presence is the shepherd of ripeness" (another translation of "I am the good shepherd," John 10:11).

This contemplation is best done in nature, but can be done any-where. Allow your eyes to close and place one hand gently on or near the physical heart. Allow your breath to slow down until your nervous system, normally engaged in the "buzz" of the out-side world, calms enough for you to sense some of the interior vibrations of the body. Allow the rhythm of your breathing and that of your heartbeat to bring you back into rhythm within. Feel that this rhythm unites not only your physical body, but also the music of your soul, your capacity to be fully yourself at any mo-ment.

Then very slowly open your eyes and notice whether you can maintain the feeling of being in rhythm as you consider the external world, with its own rhythms. Is there a deeper vibration or rhythm, a sense of ripeness, that pervades everything, inside and out?

Chapter Ten

Faces of Love: Womb, Seed, Delight

Blessedly ripe are those who radiate from a new self within;
they shall be shown a waking vision:
the womb of the One surrounding them with compassion.

—a reading of Matthew 5:7 from the Aramaic
(KJV: "Blessed are the merciful: for they shall obtain mercy.")

THE ENGLISH WORD "LOVE" HAS BECOME SO INFLUENCED BY POPULAR AND CULTURAL NOTIONS OF ROMANCE, SEXUAL POLITICS, AND CONSUMERISM THAT WE HARDLY KNOW WHAT it means anymore. Both Aramaic and Hebrew present several different words for our usual pictures of desire and love. As Jesus uses these words, all of them relate to the transformation of Hokhmah's community—the *naphsha*, or seed of the soul-self.[1]

In chapter eight we looked at the type of love with which Jesus advocates that we love Unity and our neighbor. This love was derived from the old Hebrew word for womb (*rahm*) and is related by root to "Hokhmah." It could also be translated as "compassion" or "mercy," points to an emotion that comes from the depths of one's being. Literally, it is a shining (RA) from a dense or dark interiority (ChM). The latter root also occurred in old Egyptian and subsequently made its way into Arabic, from whence we get the word al-*chem*-y. Alchemy literally means work that is done with and through the dense darkness inside. Like alchemy, the type of love called *rahm* is the end result of a process of transformation. A new self is born when the various members of a community, whether inner or outer, change and come together in a new relationship.

The fifth of the Beatitudes reported in Matthew, as I have rendered it above, reflects this birth of a new self. The Aramaic word for "shall obtain" in this Beatitude derives from the word for a waking vision or awakening,[2] and can also mean "will be shown."

This face of love results from an inner process in which one gathers and listens to the various aspects of the *naphsha*. After the small "I's," the voices of the *naphsha*, find a new relationship to the "I am," this love radiates as a natural result and one finds it radiating back from all directions. However, one cannot force this type of unconditional love. As gestation precedes physical birth, an inner alchemy must precede its outward expression. As we saw in chapter eight, Jesus taught that we first need to awaken *rahm* through devotion for what we feel is sacred in our lives. When we can feel this love reflected back to us, as though included in a ray of love from the Only Being, we can then allow the rays of *rahm* back inside, toward our subconscious selves.

The Demands of Radiant Love

The uncompromising quality of *rahm* finds expression in a saying attributed to Jesus in Matthew 10:37 (KJV):

He that loveth father or mother more than me is not worthy of me: and he that loveth son or daughter more than me is not worthy of me.

Here the word in Aramaic for "worthy"[3] can also mean to be equal to or in equilibrium with. The root of the word can mean to spread a table, make a bed, or level something that was uneven. Interpreted on the personal level, our inner work places our soul-self in equilibrium with Alaha. We prepare the self for the feast of Hokhmah. From the same root comes the name for a spiritual practice that places one in such an equilibrium with the divine: the Aramaic word for "prayer" that we encountered in chapter four. The words translated as "than me" can also mean "than with me," that is, than the way I do. So another way to hear this verse can be:

Whoever radiates with the deepest love
toward father or mother
more than the way I do
has not come into my way of
readiness and rhythm with the cosmos.
Whoever reserves more compassion,
from the womb-source of inner life,
for a son and daughter
than for the life with me
has not been prepared as I have
to be a table of compassion for Unity.

In a Middle Eastern sense, Jesus points both to himself and to his way of prayer and life here. As we saw with the "I am" statements in John, one learns the way through contact with the rhythm of the teacher. For this process, all of one's *ruhm*-love needs to be focused toward the sacred rather than dispersed. The same idea makes sense of another passage that mentions this type of womb-love (KJV):

No man can serve two masters: for either he will hate the one,
and love the other; or else he will hold to the one, and despise
the other. Ye cannot serve God and mammon. (Matthew 6:24)

The Aramaic word here for "master"[4] is the same that we saw earlier translated as "lord" in the passage on loving God and neighbor. It means literally the embodied ray of light that reminds us of Unity. The word for "serve" can also mean to labor, work, cultivate, plow, or meditate. The images unite around the notion of emptying oneself and creating a channel through effort, from the outside in. The Aramaic for "hate" comes from a root that means to strain, filter, or clarify. It is also related to the word for "moon." The word for "hold" can also mean to honor or to make heavy with burdens or possessions. The Aramaic for "despise" can also mean to neglect or consider worthless. It is related to the word for a whip or lash. Finally, "mammon" is actually a transcription of an Aramaic word (*mamona*). Its roots point to piling up outer things or appearances that become the definition of one's self or life.[5]

These additional images from the Aramaic reinforce the idea that the ray of the sacred that catches our attention asks for single-heartedness:

> *You cannot plow two rows at once,*
> *cultivate two minds in meditation,*
> *or follow two different rays back to Unity.*
> *You will either turn away from one light,*
> *like the moon waning,*
> *and shine from the depths toward the other,*
> *radiant like the sun.*
> *Or you will take up the weight of one work,*
> *honoring the burdens that come,*
> *and neglect that of the other,*
> *considering it a worthless punishment.*
> *You cannot work for Unity*
> *without being unified.*
> *You cannot cultivate the depths*
> *and simultaneously pile things up*
> *on the surface of life.*

THE CENTER HOLDS

As in the meditation at the end of chapter four, hold in focus the image of something sacred to you. You can begin the practice by gazing at a symbol, listening to music, or simply holding in feeling an image or sound that evokes the divine for you. Then, after a few moments, begin to intone the word ra-hm. *Let the resonance of this word flood your being and penetrate deeply inside. Feel your* naphsha *opening to the potential of this gift from the Source. Then simply breathe the sound and feeling of* rahm. *As you inhale, allow your self and its many small selves to absorb as much love as they can at this moment. As you exhale, allow them to radiate as much as they can at this moment.*

After a while, complete the body prayer by imagining yourself bathed in a ocean of divine love. Or imagine the universe as one continual womb of sacred creation, which gives birth to a new sense of self in you, at any and every moment.

LOVING THE ENEMY

The English and Greek versions of the Gospels use the same word for "love" in Yeshua's sayings, "Love your neighbor" and "Love your enemy." The Greek New Testament uses a form of the word *agape* for both verses—a sense of love as unconditional goodwill. The Aramaic Gospels use two different words for love here, and present a more complex view of this difficult subject. This introduces us to the second face of love that we will consider.

In the Aramaic version, both Matthew and Luke have Jesus use a form of the word *hab*[6] for "love" when he says to love your enemies.

Derived from the old Hebrew *ahabah*, this word for love can also mean to kindle a fire from something easily set ablaze, like withered leaves or dry sticks. Paradoxically, the word can also mean to grow or produce something slowly from an enclosure or from a secret place. The old Hebrew roots point to the image of a grain, or the germ of a seed, whose outer material substance (CH) covers the ability to produce fruit (AB). Both images portray *hab* as a type of love that moves from inside out. In one image it begins with small things and uses the "dead" substance of a relationship for kindling. In the other it breaks slowly through an outer shell with the force of inner creation. This force is related to the word *abwoon* (cosmic father-mother, parent, breathing life), which we looked at in chapter one. The full passage in Matthew reads like this in the King James version:

> *Love your enemies, bless them that curse you, do good to them*
> *that hate you, and pray for them which despitefully use you,*
> *and persecute you. (Matthew 5:44)*

We will take this saying phrase by phrase and expand each as fully as possible. The word for "enemies"[7] in the first phrase is the same that we saw in the parable of the wheat and tares in the previous chapter. Its roots imply domination, power, or pride taken to excess, such that one swells outwardly from an inner void or lack. As we saw in the parable, this can also point to an image of the self held past its time, or to a voice of the *naphsha* that exerts control out of proportion to its real contribution. Using these images, some additional ways to hear the first phrase are:

> *Kindle feeling slowly*
> *for that which feels excessive,*
> *out of proportion with your rhythm.*
> *Let the germ of love break*
> *gradually through the shells of pride*
> *that separate you from another,*

you from another your-self.
The husks become kindling
for a fire of new birth in which
two become one,
knowing the One behind all.

Turning to the second phrase ("bless them that curse you"), the Aramaic word translated as "bless" (*berek*)[8] can also mean to kneel or bow down. Its roots suggest the centering or the embodiment of a potential creative force. The related word *bar* means son in both Hebrew and Aramaic. The Aramaic word for "curse"[9] can also mean to cover, hide, detach, or soil something. Behind these meanings are the ideas of envelopment, seclusion, hiding, and mystery. In one sense, the "cover" provided by the insults of another (or a certain part of the self) provides the opportunity for one to go inside to a deeper aspect of self that is not affected by these insults.

Find the blessing of yielding
to those who cover you with
their own impressions,
detaching you in their minds
from who you really are.
Use this seclusion to retreat
from the surface of your image,
the pride and reputation
to which these insults stick.
Use the force to bend toward
your own deepest Self.

In the third phrase ("do good to them that hate you"), the word for "do"[10] can also mean to make or work, as well as to subdue, subject, or restrain oneself or another. Taken together, these meanings present the idea of accomplishing something by yielding. The Aramaic word translated as "good" here (*shaphira*)[11] differs from the one we investigated in the previous chapter (*taba*). *Shaphira* gives the sense of beauty and health and is related to the words for clarity as well as daybreak or the first glimmer of light. The word for "hate" is the same that we saw above in the saying on two masters: to strain, filter, or clarify. Adding these meanings, this phrase can be heard:

> *Restrain a reaction*
> *when someone helps filter out*
> *the real from the false in you.*
> *What you feel as hate is a mirror*
> *like the moon,*
> *reflecting your own self-loathing.*
> *Heal hate with beauty,*
> *inside and out.*
> *When the dawn breaks,*
> *the moon knows its time has passed.*

Looking at the fourth phrase ("pray for them which despitefully use you, and persecute you"), the word for "pray" is the same one we investigated in chapter four: to incline or bend toward, listen to, or lay a snare for. The word for "despitefully"[12] comes from a verb meaning to tie together, bind, knot, or bring together out of force or necessity. The word for "use" can also mean to lead, take, rule, or guide. The word for "persecute" (which we saw in the eighth Beatitude in chapter six) can also mean to follow, chase away, or banish. It is related by root to the verb meaning to journey, flow, or continue. The images here cluster around the idea that if we make ourselves flexible, we can use the force of seeming opposition to fuel our inner journey. With these perspectives added, this phrase can be rendered:

> *Open space for those*
> *who try to tie you up.*
> *Lay a trap that catches*

and releases all of their knots
and binding complexities.
Let your prayer for them be:
"O Alaha, use this force that
pushes and contracts,
that chases and entangles,
to guide us all back to
harmony with you."

This *ahaba* face of love continually looks for ways to bring about greater unity. It does not begin from an unconditional, radiant place, as does *rahm*. Instead, it works gradually toward *rahm* at the same time that one works with one's inner self. Another way to put this is that in *ahabah*-love one sees outer conditions and events as a mirror. In *rahm*-love the mirror disappears and one shines equally, like the sun, on those who respond and those who don't. Significantly, immediately following the above saying in Matthew, Jesus speaks about the sun shining on the "just and the unjust."

ALAHA LOOKS FOR OPPORTUNITIES TO LOVE

The whole of Sacred Unity participates in *ahabah*—this gradually kindled love and transformation. It looks constantly for opportunities to bring this love into the least loving situations. In the translation of John 3:16 that we considered in chapter eight, the whole Universe yearns with *ahabah* toward those who can embody this integration in their lives. John also reports another saying of Yeshua where this type of mysteriously growing *ahabah*-love is mentioned (KJV):

This is my commandment, That ye love one another, as I have loved you. Greater love hath no man than this, that a man lay down his life for his friends. (John 15:12-13)

In this passage, the Aramaic word for "commandment"[13] comes from a word meaning to visit, inspect, inquire, or review regularly. It can also mean to judge, depart, or bequeath. The word's roots indicate an alternating, pendulum-like movement that stirs the substance through which it passes. The word for "life" is again *naphsha*, the inner self. The word for "friend" (*rahma*) is derived from *rahm*, the first, unconditional face of love. One yields one's images of the *naphsha*, even lets them die, in order to pursue the path on which this type of love takes one. The goal is complete unity—between all aspects of the self, and between one and One. Anything less may need to be sacrificed along the way:

> *This is my bequest to you—*
> *let it measure you regularly,*
> *stirring you to review your life:*
> *Just as I have kindled a big fire*
> *from leaves and twigs in you,*
> *just as a seed led you to*
> *full-bloomed love for me,*
> *use the small and weak*
> *to kindle and grow the*
> *mystery of love for each other*
> *and for the "other" parts of self.*
> *The most powerful way*
> *to love like this asks you to*
> *sacrifice your images*
> *of who you think you are,*
> *to work inside before*
> *you respond outside,*
> *to feel Alaha's impatience for love*
> *in your own.*

In the Aramaic Gospels, Yeshua uses a form of *ahabah* wherever he uses the formula: "do this as I have done it"; for instance, "As the Father hath loved me, so have I loved you: continue ye in my love" (KJV: John 15:9). This parallel phrasing points to the overall images of yielding and expanding, receiving and giving that provide the keynote of *ahabah*. Unlike *rahm*, *ahabah* needs a giver and receiver. Like a seed that breaks open, the love of *ahabah* arises from the nature of the particle-cosmos—earth—to embody itself in diversity. The love of *rahm* operates more in the wave realm, that is, heaven.

DESIRE AND DELIGHT

As we proceed along the paths of love in either sense, we also run into the energy of passionate desire. Aramaic has two words that give another view of this experience as well.

We saw the first word for desire in the fourth line of the prayer of Jesus considered in chapter seven (usually translated, "Let thy will be done on earth as it is in heaven.") Besides "will," the Aramaic word *sebyana*[14] can also mean desire, delight, or wish. Its roots point to something that swells or rises, follows a certain harmony, and moves like a large crowd or a host of stars. This force unites wave and particle realities. It exemplifies the harmony of the cosmic spheres, which move in their appointed courses simply because it is their deepest purpose and delight to do so. We might not even call this a type of love, except that it expresses the deepest calling of our being when we are in tune with the cosmos. When Yeshua says "Thy will be done" in Gethsemane,[15] he asks that this power of desire support him. Other ways to hear this phrase can be:

> Let your delight be,
> Your desire be,
> Your whole unfolding harmony

be and move through me,
as individual as a moment of pleasure,
as cosmic as my place in the stars.

There may be no more powerful prayer than this one. With either of the previous types of love, we may still maintain the illusion that we are in control. Not so here. This desire-power also fuels Yeshua's healing work. For instance, near the beginning of his ministry, a man with a skin disease says to him, "If you are willing, you can cleanse me."[16] Yeshua responds *"Saba ana!"* or "I have the desire-power: it is in tune with heaven and earth." Conversely, in the Aramaic version, the guests who decline the invitation to dinner in Yeshua's parable reportedly have no *sebyana.*[17]

The other Aramaic word for desire, *'eshkah,* is imported from old Hebrew, and as a verb is usually translated "find."[18] In the Song of Songs, the corresponding Hebrew word points to a force of passionate and erotic desire. The Aramaic form appears in the "seek and find" passage that we looked at briefly in chapter four.[19] *'Eshkah* can also mean to invent, discover, or recover. The roots imply an embodied form of the sacred heat or fire, a force that regenerates nature each season. For instance, when Jesus says that he has not "found" any greater faith than that of the centurion,[20] this word reminds one that nothing can happen or be found without the universe's heat and fire behind it. *'Eshkah* also appears in the following saying from Matthew 7:14,[21] where the King James version translates it as "find":

Because strait is the gate, and narrow is the way, which leadeth unto life, and few there be that find it.

Here the word for "strait"[22] can also mean thin, frail, subtle, delicate, keen, or ethereal. The word for "gate" derives from a verb meaning to flow or open. We saw the same root used in the word "ethphatah" in the story of Jesus healing the deaf and dumb man. This type of opening allows one to go over or through boundaries. Again, the door is one between the worlds, so to speak.

The Aramaic word for "narrow"[23] can also mean afflicted and comes from a verb meaning to compel, constrain, press, or make urgent. We saw the word for "way" (*urha*) earlier in chapter four when we considered the saying "I am the way, the truth, and the life." It can mean a path or a manner of living and is related by root to the type of light called *nur*, which we considered in chapter five. This straight-line light of intelligence becomes embodied as a path, literally or figuratively. As we saw in chapter nine, the word for "few" comes from a verb meaning to diminish, lessen, or be reduced in strength. In the context of the soul-self, the word means to be faint-hearted. The word for "life"(*hayye*) is the one for life energy that we considered in the previous chapter. So with Aramaic ears we might also hear:

> Subtle and delicate is the door
> that lets us float between the worlds,
> over our boundaries and beyond.
> Compelling and urgent is the way
> that shows the light connecting
> us with the energy of the cosmos.
> It is not a way for the faint-hearted,
> for those who do not use their full inner fire
> of passionate desire to find it.

The paths of love and desire down which life takes us may lead to some confusing places. According to the Song of Songs, this confusion is a preparation for the life we face after our physical bodies return to dust, and when only the waves of love persist—the love that is as strong as death.[24]

An Abundance of Love

Return to the sense of breathing in the heart. Allow the feeling in the heart to spiral out to include the womb-center in the belly and then the whole body. Breathe in and out ra-hm, *feeling radiant love for the divine in all the ways that it touches you most deeply. Then allow this womb-love to flood Hokhmah's neighborhood, your* naphsha, *with as much unconditional love as it can absorb. After some moments, breathe in and out* aha-bah, *feeling the give and take of love, the yielding and overcoming, as it plays itself out in your friendships, conflicts, and other relationships. Finally, after some moments, breathe in and out* saba ana: "*I have the desire-power. The pleasure of the cosmos works through all of me.*" *Give thanks for the ability to experience this pleasure.*

Chapter Eleven

Yeshua bar Alaha

Whatever house you enter,
let your first words be:
"Shalama bayta:"
Peace to this house and family—
May it complete its purpose
and tell its tale to the end.
May it fulfill itself in surrender
to the One.

> —a reading from the Aramaic of Luke 10:5,
> with a parallel at Matthew 10:12-13
> (KJV: "And into whatsoever house ye shall
> enter, first say, Peace be to this house.")

WHO WAS YESHUA? IN THE JOURNEY WE HAVE TAKEN THROUGH VARIOUS THEMES OF HIS TEACHING, WE HAVE SEEN IN HIM RESONANCES WITH BOTH THE MYTHIC first human in Jewish cosmology—Adam—and with Hokhmah, Holy Wisdom. We have seen that he spoke about Sacred Unity in the form of spirit-breath, holiness-spaciousness, light-intelligence, and heaven and earth in ways that a person raised with a Semitic view of the universe would understand. At the same time, he challenged the conventional way that these concepts were interpreted by the ruling powers of his time. We can see him as mystic and prophet at the same time. Heard with Hebrew-Aramaic ears, the "kingdom" and new community he spoke of appear as both inner and outer. The morality he taught reemphasized the root meanings of good and evil as ripe and unripe. He used the nuances of various Aramaic words for love to reveal love's different faces of compassion, relationship, and passion.

None of this, however, gives us an answer to the following questions: Was his birth divine or human? What was he doing before he set out on the career reported in the Gospels? Was he, or did he see himself as, the Jewish messiah? And if so, what would that have meant—an earthly kingdom or an apocalyptic, heavenly one? How much of the Gospel language that refers to the person of Jesus was added later, to emphasize views of him in which various early Christian groups were invested?

THE PARTICLE APPROACH

There are at least two ways to approach these questions. The first uses Western historical-critical means to decipher which threads of the Gospels can be distinguished as the points of view of various early Christian groups. Theoretically, when all of these threads have been identified, what is left will be closest to what the earliest communities believed, and thus closest to what Jesus himself actually said and did. As this type of scholarship has progressed over the past hundred years, what remains of the proposed "authentic" Jesus tradition has become smaller and smaller. Biblical scholars now not only speak about a hypothetical Q source but also of a "pre-Q" tradition or traditions. Ultimately, the first transmission was oral: in the beginning was the spoken and remembered word. And of course there is no historical record of this. With less and less actual text to work with, the various scholars hypothesize about the historical Jesus in various ways, each according to her or his favorite theme: the Greek cynic, the peasant magician, the apocalyptic prophet, and so forth.

If the overall thrust of this seems familiar, that is because during the twentieth century researchers in physics have engaged in a similar search for the so-called elementary particle, the building block of all matter. As the means of measurement get better, the particles measured become smaller and smaller. Related to this, a basic finding of the new physics has been that the way a particle or interaction is viewed and measured determines the way it behaves. The act of observing actually changes what is observed, because the observer is part of the same field. The basic principle of Einstein's relativity theory—that matter and energy are interchangeable—has been supplemented by the observation that light can behave both as a particle and as a wave. When one uses "particle" methods to measure, light behaves like a particle. When one uses "wave" methods, it behaves like a wave.

The same is true of research into the "historical Jesus." In general, it plays by "particle" rules. The way it defines a fact and defines history itself determines what it finds, or doesn't find. In the terms of the inter-related dyad of heaven and earth discussed in this book, the Western historical perspective represents an "earth" view of things. It can be useful, but it is only one side of the picture.

THE WAVE APPROACH

The "heaven" way of looking at things views the wisdom tradition of Jesus, his acts and words, according to a "wave" approach. If we look at the overall flow, breath, rhythm, and tenor of the core sayings and stories of Jesus in both the canonical Gospels and in early writings like the Gospel of Thomas, we can develop a *feeling* not only for who Jesus was, but also who he is in our inner life. This is not a matter of what Jesus *means*, in a factual or theological sense, but of what his *shem*, or vibration, activates in us. Which aspects of his wisdom teachings can we embody in everyday life? In this book I have been arguing for, and hopefully demonstrating, the validity and usefulness of such "wave" methods. I believe that these methods accord with a traditional Middle Eastern approach to the words of a mystic or prophet. They also more closely approximate the way the early Christian oral tradition understood Jesus: as a living presence rather than a dead historical figure.[1]

If we use these means, we can allow for various changes to Yeshua's words made by later editors. We can even allow for the possibility that Yeshua did not say or do a particular thing. Like the way physicists view what is called a quantum field, we know that the heart of what we are looking for, the heart of Jesus if you will, is within a certain sphere of feeling and experience. The approach I have been illustrating offers one door into this quantum field of a native, Middle Eastern Jesus. With our own heart and life experience we can look at his words and acts, and touch the mythic, living reality of Yeshua in the same way that inspired people in the earliest Middle Eastern Jesus movements.[2]

JESUS BEFORE HERESY

The earliest followers of Jesus were not divided into authentic, orthodox "Christians" and inauthentic, heterodox heretics. This view of history was written by the winners. Unlike the later Christian church, the earliest Jesus movements seem to have emphasized Jesus' words of wisdom and his teaching ministry, rather than his origin and his end. His words and actions as a prophet and mystic inspired them to incorporate his way of being in their own lives. They repeated his words from memory, as those of a living rather than a historical reality.

Questions I have left unanswered in this book are also ones that these early Christians considered secondary to their practice, that is, questions about Jesus' birth, death, and resurrection.[3] Whatever views they held about his divinity and humanity, they held them within the overall Jewish concept of God as Unity. The questions that primarily concerned them were ones of practice, not theology. For instance, was it desirable for those who followed Yeshua to continue to attend the synagogue or not?

Many Westerners tend to see other people's religions as myths, but do not understand either the mythic dimension of their own religion or secular philosophy, or the power that it carries. A Western view of history as a collection of particular facts, seen or interpreted in hindsight, does not define ultimate truth. A prophet or mystic either touches one's heart or does not. Throughout history, the primary vehicle for this touch has been the oral handing down of that person's words, stories, actions, and spiritual practices. These "wave" methods empower most of the devotional energy on this planet.[4] The same methods, by other names, also empower philosophies and beliefs not considered religious, such as nationalism, agnosticism, and secular humanism.

When we take the long view of Western Christianity, we can also see the beauty that has arisen from doctrines like the Incarnation, the Trinity, and the Resurrection as they have been interpreted by the artists, poets, and mystics of the last fifteen hundred years. Hildegard of Bingen, Meister Eckhart, Bach, Mozart, Teresa of Avila, Michelangelo, Dante and many others were not motivated by theological, "particle"-method dissections of Jesus' historical career, or the exact determination of his human and divine nature. Instead, they were empowered by the mythic energy of the stories and sayings they learned by ear and heart. As they were memorized, these stories and sayings became part of them, rather than remaining objects outside them. This "wave"-method, intuitive approach to Jesus' teachings inspired their creativity, and these contributions of the great saints and mystics have inspired creativity in many others.

I will consider this book effective if it leads to more art, music, poetry, healing, inspired living, and lifelong learning based in love.

SON OF MAN

We can turn our attention now to two phrases that appear in the Gospels in the mouth of Jesus or others, and to which enormous significance has been assigned over the centuries: "son of man" and "son of God." We must allow for the possibility that these words were inserted later into the stories and sayings reported in canonical Gospels. However, we can also look at their possible implications when viewed through the Hebrew and Aramaic languages.

Because virtually all translations into European languages capitalize the phrase "Son of Man," we have come to take for granted that this expression is a sacred title. But while we know the expression became a title in early Christianity, there is no evidence for its use as a title for a divine or messianic figure, or even as a form of address, before or during the time of Jesus. Its only appearance in the Jewish scriptures occurs in a vision of Daniel (7:13): "behold, one like the Son of man came with the clouds of heaven, and came to the Ancient of days, and they brought him near before him" (KJV).

Even here we cannot be sure that the version we have of the book of Daniel was put into final form before the synoptic Gospels were written. In addition, the phrase is not used as a title in Daniel, but simply as another term for human being—its usual use in Hebrew. A similar term, "son of *adam*," is found frequently in Ezekiel.[5] Both the Daniel and Ezekiel passages influenced an early Jewish mystical practice in which the aspirant attempted to ascend through the heavenly realms and attain a vision of the Holy One's throne or chariot. According to some scholars, these practices were already in existence by the time of Jesus.[6]

As the canonical Gospels have it, the phrase "son of man" is only uttered by Jesus himself, never about him by others. There seems to be no objection to his use of it by anyone around him (whereas there is certainly objection to many other things that he says and does). Further, there is no equivalent phrase in Greek, so most biblical scholars reason that the Greek version of the Gospels must have translated a phrase originally in Aramaic or Hebrew. The puzzle about the significance of the phrase becomes more complex because in a number of parallel passages in the Gospels, the expression seems to be simply a substitute for "I." For instance, Jesus' question to his disciples (KJV): "Whom do men say that I, the Son of man, am?"(Matthew 16:13), is recorded in Matthew, Mark, and Luke, but only Matthew uses "the son of man." In other cases, who the expression refers to is more ambiguous, for instance in the following:

> For the son of man is lord even of the sabbath day. (Matthew 12:8)[7]

> But that ye may know that the Son of man hath power on earth to forgive sins (then saith he to the sick of the palsy,) Arise, and take up thy bed, and go unto thine house. (Matthew 9:6)[8]

In these cases as well as others, if we substitute the words "human being" for "son of man," regarding it as a common Aramaic usage instead of a title for Jesus, the meaning changes dramatically.

George Lamsa commented that according to Eastern Christian understanding, "son of man" simply means "human being, an ordinary man." He felt that Jesus used it as a sort of anti-title to upset the expectations of people that he should have a noble upbringing or assert a claim to royal descent traceable to his family lineage:

> When an Oriental declines honors and homage, he says, I do not deserve this honor. I am nothing, I am just a man, a plain working man. In the east, men of rank and nobility are addressed according to their social standing and rank and given the title of Mare, my lord. Religious men are always honored and called Rabbi or father. A peasant is called a man.[9]

We can also look at the Aramaic expression bar nasha itself. Here

we find that *nasha* means any human being, man or woman, and derives from the Hebrew-Aramaic root NSh, which points to something
weak and subject to change. Another form of the word in Aramaic means
to forget. This is a view of the human being as part of the limited, individual, "earth" reality. The word translated as "son" (*bar*) has root connections to the word for light-intelligence (*aor*) that we investigated in
chapter five. This word reminds one that all relatedness stems from the
original divine light, or the "heaven" reality.

Viewed in this way, the term *bar nasha* expresses a combination of
"earth" and "heaven" meanings. This could provide a way to read the
above passages in a more mystical sense. For instance, the definition
and impression of sins or mistakes, as well as the rules of the Sabbath,
are based in a transitory reality—in the earthly, particle world. As human beings, we are based in that world but also participate in the heaven-
light world, and so we have power over human-produced rules and impressions.

In the Gospel of Thomas we find that Yeshua uses the expression
"son of man" to mean fully human or complete, in the way we saw in
chapter nine. For instance:

> *Jesus said: When you make the two into one, you shall become*
> *sons of man, and when you say, "Mountain, be moved," it will*
> *be moved.* (Saying 106)

Son of God

When we look at the expression "son of God," we find a very different story. Jesus uses the expression only a few times in John, and
never in Matthew, Mark, or Luke. When he is asked directly whether
he is the Christ, the Son of God, by the high priest in Jerusalem (Matthew 26:63), he answers ambiguously and then seems to quote from
the passage in Daniel above. The question of who witnessed and re-

ported this occurrence again raises the question about the strand of Gospel tradition we are dealing with.

If we use the "wave" approach I advocate, we need to investigate whether there can be a sense of "son of God" that first, may not be a royal or divine title exclusive to Jesus, and second, can provide meaning for us.

To answer the first question, we can look again to what we know of the earliest Jewish Christianity, before the complex doctrines of the Trinity were formulated. Those Christians honored Yeshua variously: as God's suffering servant, as the last prophet and ultimate interpreter of Jewish law, and as the embodiment of Hokhmah. In this so-called "low Christology," the expression "son of God" meant an adopted son of Alaha, not the exclusive one. In particular, Yeshua exemplified the way that any human being could consciously realize her or himself as an adopted child of Unity.[10]

For the purposes of our own spiritual life, what is shown to be earlier may not necessarily be more useful. The question is: is it more meaningful? To be a child of Alaha in the way that Jesus mentions in the seventh Beatitude in Matthew 5:9 means literally to be a planter of peace (*shalama*).[11] The Aramaic for "they shall be called the children of God" means literally "they shall be hollowed out, or become channels for Unity."[12] Both images—planting and digging—convey the necessity of exerting oneself to prepare a space for Oneness. As children of humanity (*nasha*), we are naturally forgetful of our connections with each other and with the sacred, and need to work to make these connections conscious. As children of Unity, we have to work hard to make space for the divine to flow through us, as it is meant to do.

Both of these images recall the description in the old Jewish creation story of human beings as *adam*—beings through whom the blood, sap, juice, or essence of the divine can flow. Although in the Aramaic version of the Gospels Jesus does not use the term "son of *adam*," I find it entirely possible that he may have done so, as it unites elements of both "son of man" and "son of God." And as we have seen, a number of other sayings and stories of Jesus point to a spiritual practice that asks us to relive the experience of the first human being.

BLOOD AND BODY

The theme of the first human being also allows us to see other possible interpretations of the words of Jesus at the Passover celebration on the night before he was crucified. Matthew reports them this way (KJV):

> And he took a cup, and gave thanks, and gave it to them, saying, Drink ye all of it; for this is my blood of the covenant, which is poured out for many unto remission of sins. But I say unto you, I shall not drink henceforth of this fruit of the vine, until that day when I drink it new with you in my Father's kingdom. (Matthew 26:27-29)[13]

The Aramaic language provides only one word for "blood." This is dama,[14] a word which, like the Hebrew word dam, must also stand for juice, wine, sap, and essence. It shares the same root with the word adam. So Jesus may have been saying, this is my blood, juice, wine, sap, or essence. The reference in the above sentence to "fruit of the vine" emphasizes the multiple meanings of dama. Further, the word for "fruit" can also mean any offspring, including human. The word for "vine" comes from the verb meaning to dig, or form a body from. Metaphorically, it can be used in Hebrew or Aramaic to refer to a blood lineage, for instance, the vine sprung from Adam or Abraham.[15]

The resonance to adam, the first human, makes sense of many of these possible meanings. As we remember our pristine nature as primal human beings, we can also release subsequent mistakes or offenses made by ourselves or others. This practice of forgiveness is intoxicating "wine," as is the practice of reliving the creation story—being "born from the first becoming." In addition, we can see the meaning of *dama* as "blood" in relation to forgiveness. Blood releases us, heartbeat-by-heartbeat, breath-by-breath, from the physical impressions of the past. The potential to forgive ourselves and others is just as close, immediate, and ever-present as is our blood.

From this view of his Aramaic words, we could see Jesus here initiating a new ritual, which in addition to the Passover ritual of remembering the Jewish freedom from bondage in Egypt, recalled the mythic origin of his listeners as primal humans, before the divisions of "chosen" and "non-chosen" people even existed. In later Christianity, this ritual was called Eucharist or Communion, but was largely interpreted as symbolizing Jesus' suffering and death on the cross in redemption of the sins of humanity. The Jewish roots of the ritual were ignored.

Matthew continues his report of this incident (KJV):

And as they were eating, Jesus took bread, and blessed it, and broke it; and gave it to the disciples, and said, Take, eat, this is my body. (Matthew 26:26)[16]

Here the Aramaic word for "body,"[17] which we saw in chapter five when considering the saying about the "light of the body," means a corpse, or something that gradually loses heat and energy over a period of time. This is the most common word for body that Jesus uses in the Aramaic Gospels. This word reminds one that the body has only a limited life span compared to the longer-lived soul-self (*naphsha*) and breath-spirit (*ruha*).

When Yeshua identifies the bread (*lakhma*) with his dead body, we can also see him indirectly invoking Hokhmah, as we saw in chapter seven. Holy Wisdom produces food for our consumption that is ultimately made up of the dead bodies of other beings, including human ones after they return to the earth. In this sense, we can see that Yeshua both foretells his impending death as well as implies the ultimate equality of all bodies in the eyes of Wisdom.

The Coptic Gospel of Thomas quotes Yeshua making a similar reference to a corpse, which accords with the Aramaic sense of "body" expressed above. In this case, he tells his students to find a place within themselves—*naphsha* or *ruha*—that will outlast their bodies:

> *You, too, look for a place for yourselves in repose (or invigorated rest), otherwise you will become a corpse and be eaten.* (Saying 60:6)

Again, in contrast or in addition to the Passover ritual, the bread shared is not only the bread of suffering (as experienced by the Jewish people in Egypt) but also the bread of Holy Wisdom, who issues an invitation to a common table. At least two examples of this mythic invitation occur in the Jewish Wisdom tradition current in Jesus' time:

> *Come and eat my bread, drink the wine which I have mixed.* (Spoken by Wisdom in Proverbs 9:5)

> *She [Wisdom] will give him the bread of understanding to eat, and the water of wisdom to drink.* (Sirach 15:3)

THE GREETING OF PEACE

Yeshua's greeting of peace, with which this chapter begins, reinforces the themes we have seen above, which remind us of what persists and what dies in our human existence. While the Western definition of the word "peace" sees it simply as the absence of war or conflict, the Semitic languages see it as something more profound. Both the Hebrew *shalom* and the Aramaic *shalama* derive from a verb that means to be fulfilled or complete, to surrender or be delivered, or to die.

The convergence of these images may again be found in the Jewish creation story, where Genesis reports that on the seventh day God "rested." The Hebrew word for rest, *shabath*, can also mean to end or complete something, as well as to restore oneself to an original state or point of departure. By a mystical interpretation of this passage, as Unity rested, it restored to itself the remembrance of what had been before creation, the primal void. This period of remembrance was sanctified— space was reserved for it—as the day of rest, or Sabbath.

When one greets another with *shalom, shalama,* or *salaam* (the Arabic form), it can be an instant of Sabbath. Both people have the opportunity to remember their origins as beings whose beginning is ultimately a mystery. This remembrance can help clear away a history of offenses given, received, and perceived. It can produce peace on a very deep level, not by invoking certainty or idealism, but by bringing awareness of uncertainty and the ultimate mortality of all forms.

Not to know one's origins ultimately results in doubt. Recognizing our origins can mean the realization of our human ancestry as *bar nasha*, children of change, or it can mean acknowledgment of the origins of the universe. To feel one's mortality can bring desolation; the uncertainty and tenuousness of human existence can motivate an impulsive search for control and acquisition, as a way to keep the uncertainty at bay. Or it can engender an appreciation for the preciousness of each interaction—each one an opportunity to remember the peace that existed before the story of the universe began.

AN INNER SHALOM

Return to a quiet place of breathing awareness, feeling the word shalom *or* shalama *riding on the inhalation and exhalation. With this feeling and word, feel the presence of Hokhmah, Holy Wisdom, and greet each aspect of your inner self that you meet. As much as possible, allow each one to participate in feeling the mysterious origins of the universe. Invite each aspect of your self to a table of bread and wine that can fulfill the ultimate desire of each to bring its purpose into being. As you end the meditation, look into the days immediately ahead of you. In what ways can this greeting and invitation enter your interactions with everyone and everything you meet?*

Afterword

The Hidden Gospel and the Historical Jesus

W HILE *The Hidden Gospel* is primarily a work of spiritual inspiration and teaching, I believe that its approach is also grounded in and makes a contribution to biblical studies.

From a Western viewpoint, the work of this book takes place in the formal field of study called hermeneutics, the science of interpretation.[1] But to approach interpretation from a Middle Eastern viewpoint means that one must combine many areas of study, like psychology and cosmology, which have become divorced from religion and the study of sacred texts in the European tradition.

I have already noted some of the benefits and drawbacks of certain historical-critical approaches. Essentially, they are only one part of the picture. From the standpoint of Western scholarship, I place my work in another school of interpretation sometimes known as "reader response." This school maintains that we must look at a particular text as a whole, in the way in which a reader (past or present) might understand it. What we bring to a text as a reader has as much to do with what we see as the text itself. As a supplement to the approach of the Western reader response school, I have added the *midrashic* concept of translation and interpretation as a spiritual practice, accompanied by prayer, including body prayer and chant. What is commonly called reader response in modern biblical scholarship becomes "experiencer response" in my work.

One sees something similar to the mystical tradition of Jewish *midrash* in the variety of interpretations given to the words and actions

171

of Yeshua by the various Jesus movement groups that formed after his passing. This variety continued during the transition from an oral to a written transmission of Jesus' words and actions. I believe that a *midrashic* approach most closely approximates what it would have been like to hear and meditate upon the words of Jesus in an oral culture. The circular and spiral methods of interpretation employed in this book, combined with spiritual practice and meditation, attempt to recreate—as well as a written work can in the postmodern era—what it would have been like to sit at the feet of a teacher in the Middle East. This approach may be seen as idiosyncratic, but it is precisely the unique and unexpected element in interpretation that distinguishes the commentary given by a spiritual teacher in the Middle East from one given by a text-based academic using linear methods.

I also see the *midrashic* approach as firmly grounded in social science research theory, as I demonstrated in a paper I gave at the International Meeting of the Society of Biblical Literature in 1998.[2] Various social science research theories of inquiry suggest that since the observer is always part of the field that includes what she or he is studying, there is no such thing as complete objectivity in research. At the same time, one can go beyond mere subjectivity by considering the object studied from many different viewpoints. This involves including one's own preconceptions as part of the study, along with the views of others, as well as the "data" itself. Based on this, one can define what is "valid" or "true" as that which is useful for a particular group at a given time. In that paper I proposed what I called a "hermeneutics of indeterminacy," which provides a meeting place for *midrash* and social science theory.

This model proposes that the biblical scholar must undertake the type of introspective work that a psychologist or social scientist would to "clean the lens" of her or his perspective. It proposes also that the personal spiritual experiences of biblical scholars have as much to do with what they see (or don't see) in a text that deals with spiritual experience as any linear methods they use. *The Hidden Gospel* makes a contribution to the overall field of biblical hermeneutics in that I have demonstrated here how such an approach to interpreting the words of Jesus can be undertaken.

Some people will say that what I am providing is essentially a gnostic or Sufi look at the words of Jesus. I am willing to grant this with several reservations. As far as what is called gnosticism goes, most scholars now agree that this tradition was present in the Middle East at and before the time of Jesus. Many of its elements are interchangeable with various Jewish mystical traditions of his day—for instance, *merkabah* (throne-chariot) and *bereshit* (creation) mysticism, as well as the Hokhmah wisdom tradition. All of these are more likely to have been influences on Jesus as other traditions that have been proposed, such as the Greek cynic school. In addition, the term "gnostic" itself has been challenged by many scholars as a convenient label for practices that came to be seen as nonorthodox in later manifestations of either Christianity or Judaism. If we can no longer call the Gospel of Thomas "gnostic," as many scholars now maintain, then we must reevaluate the use of this term entirely.[3]

I have shown how a reading of the Aramaic Peshitta version of the (primarily) Q and Mark sayings and stories of Jesus correlates with a Semitic reading of Thomas. A number of scholars have also pointed out relationships between the Jesus of Thomas and of John; these have also figured in my presentation. The result reveals a "historical Jesus" as likely as those previously proposed: Jesus as a Middle Eastern mystic. I believe that this view of Jesus is valid if it helps bring the reader or hearer into a closer, living relationship with her or his own spirituality.

As far as my own beliefs go, I see no reason why the standard of biblical scholarship should be set at the extreme of either skepticism or dogmatic belief. There are more possible options for rigorous work than these. Nor do I see why one needs to be either an agnostic or a Christian believer in the Western sense to do biblical scholarship. In short, I don't see why a Middle Eastern spiritual practitioner should be excluded from this work.

As a practicing Sufi, I am not interested in proving or even implying that anything Jesus said or did prefigures Mohammed, although some Muslims may maintain this. I put this type of interpretation (which has been called supercessionist) in the same category as Christians using the Jewish scriptures solely as a source for possible predictions of Jesus' mission.

Although there are differences among Sufis as well, this Sufi and many others point to the injunction of the Quran itself for justification of deep study of the Bible. Jesus is given a high place of honor in the Quran and is mentioned more often than any other prophet, always in a positive light.[4] Jesus is said to have been taught by Sacred Unity "the Book and the Wisdom and the Torah and the Gospel" (Sura 5:113). His actual message is not repeated in the Quran, and the reader is expected to search the Jewish and Christian bibles themselves.

Further, the Quran states that an ancient, original religion existed prior to any names and forms—a religion of the *hanif:*

> *So turn your face and your purpose toward the primordial religion of the upright (hanif)—the original nature in which the One created all humanity. Let there be no change in this ancient, self-sustaining religion, created by the Only Being, which is the standard (qayyim) of all religions. But most among humanity do not understand.* (Sura 30:30)[5]

According to the Quran, each culture has historically received a messenger or prophet who exemplified this primordial message of the sacred, which is behind all the cultural and political forms of orthodox religion. For instance:

The Only Being has opened to you the way of religion that the One commended to Noah to follow. It is the same faith that we have revealed to you and that we showed to Abraham, Moses, and Jesus, so that true religion might continue in the earth. Do not divide not yourselves into sects. (Sura 42:13)

Each community has a messenger, and when its messenger comes, judgment is given among them by that messenger with justice. (Sura 10:48)

You [Mohammed] are only a warner; every people has its own guide. (Sura 13: 8)

It then behooves a Sufi to prove these sayings of the Quran by finding and honoring the wisdom in all traditions and by making it applicable to everyday life.

Acknowledgments

My special thanks go to my life partner, Kamae A. Miller, for her support through the writing of this book and for her critical editorial help. For feedback and ongoing dialogue about the nature of the Aramaic Jesus, I would also like to thank my two collaborators in the Jesus and Ecology Project, Dr. Joseph Grabill of Illinois State University-Normal and Deborah Oberg of the Association of Humanistic Psychology. For support for my attempts to bring this work to the attention of the scholarly community, I would like to thank my colleagues in the Society of Biblical Literature, especially those in the international branch of the History of Interpretation Section, as well as my colleagues in the American Academy of Religion, especially fellow members of the steering committee of the Mysticism Group. For financial support for my research, I would like to thank the many contributors to the Abwoon Study Circle, a community that gathers at a number of retreats worldwide as well as at a virtual meeting place: http://www.abwoon.com. For spiritual guidance, I thank my own guide in the Sufi tradition, Murshid Moineddin Jablonski, as well as my spiritual grandmother and grandfather, Murshida Aziza and Pir Hidayat Inayat Khan. Finally, I would like to thank my editor at Quest Books, Brenda Rosen, as well as my agent and former editor, Tom Grady, for their confidence in this project and their willingness to invest time and energy in bringing it to birth.

Notes

Note: A date in parentheses after an author's name refers to the date of publication of the work cited as listed in the bibliography. The number in parentheses after the transliteration of an Aramaic word refers to the number of that entry in the glossary. My two previous books are abbreviated as POC (*Prayers of the Cosmos*) and DW (*Desert Wisdom*).

Introduction

1. See "No Jews or Christians in the Bible," by Dr. John J. Pilch (1998), p. 3.
2. The composition date of the Gospel of Thomas has been estimated in the first century CE, making at least the core of it as old or older than the canonical Gospels. For instance, see Stephen J. Patterson (1998).
3. See Küng (1993), pp. 123-124. Küng comments elsewhere, "I wonder: if a Muslim or Jew should be expected to recognize the Hellenist councils from Nicaea to Chalcedon, what would Jesus of Nazareth, the Jew, have done?" (p. 95).
4. In *A Wandering Aramean: Collected Aramaic Essays*, Joseph Fitzmyer, S.J. (1979) moves this date back to the eighth century BCE. He also maintains that a type of "postbiblical Hebrew" did survive the captivities of the sixth century in some areas, but that Aramaic was the most common spoken language of first-century CE Palestine. See p. 29ff.
5. This raises the question of why no definitive manuscripts exist, in any language, of what Jesus said and did. This has much to do with the development of Western Christianity, as I show in the first chapter. It also has to do with the way words proceed from an oral to a written transmission. In ancient times, an oral culture of memorized words and stories was much more predominant than it is today. The linear nature of written texts is not the same as the more circular or fluid dynamics of oral transmission. For more on the differences between oral and written culture in relation to the Gospels, see the work of Werner Kelber, who began in the early 80s what is now a heated discussion with his book *The Oral and the Written Gospel* (1997).
6. This was attempted by biblical scholar C. C. Torrey earlier in this century (1933 and 1936).

Chapter One: The Hidden Gospel

1. See Elaine Pagels (1979).

2. Several feminist scholars have pointed out that this largely affected women. See, for instance, Joanna Dewey (1994).

3. A thoughtful and literate account of these developments appears in Karen Armstrong's *A History of God* (1993).

4. Ata'ur-Raliem, Muhammad and Ahmad Thomson (1996). *Jesus: Prophet of Islam*. London: Ta-Ha Publishers, Ltd.

5. For a social history of early Christian persecution and the various communities that demonized one another, see Pagels (1995), especially pp. 112-148.

6. A concise critique of the whole historical Jesus enterprise from a phenomenological standpoint is made by biblical scholar Luke Timothy Johnson (1998), pp. 12-26. In addition, the Q hypothesis is currently challenged by an alternative one, usually called the two notebook hypothesis. This proposes that oral remembrances of Jesus' words and acts were collected in two different early summaries that were used as the basis for teaching. For instance, see Wilson (1997).

7. Unfortunately, the picture reversed itself once Constantine Christianized the Roman Empire. Then the Persians began to sporadically persecute the Christians in these lands as well. For stories of early martyrs of Eastern Christianity, see Sebastian P. Brock and Susan Ashbrook Harvey (1987).

8. Early versions of the Peshitta delete the books of 2 Peter, 2 and 3 John, Jude, and Revelation. Significantly, they place the epistles of James, Peter, and John, which express a more Jewish version of early Christianity, after Acts and before the Pauline epistles.

9. Rihbany, (1916), pp. 404, 410.

10. For other possibilities see POC pp. 12-14, and DW, p. 249.

11. Some scholars (for instance, Crossan, 1994b) have proposed that a shorter version of a saying of Jesus may be closer to the original oral tradition. However, this presupposes the short memory and attention span present in modern and postmodern cultures. All evidence shows that people in oral cultures had excellent memories, and that the language remembered in stories and sayings held a higher degree of complexity than written language. See, for instance, Lings (1992) and Fine (1992).

12. See, for instance, Kanagaraj (1998).

CHAPTER TWO: ALAHA

1. God: 'alāhā (47).

2. The E and A can both be transliterations of the first letter of the Hebrew or Aramaic alphabet, *aleph*.

3. Heart: lebā (54).

4. For the translations of the Gospel of Thomas from the Coptic, I am relying on and sometimes combining two scholarly versions, each of which takes various liberties with gaps in the text, based upon their own interpretations. These two are Guillaumont, Puech, Quispel, Till, and Al Masih, trans. (1959); and Bethage et. al, in Stephen Patterson and James Robinson (1998). The latter contains a new English translation by the authors in conjunction with the Berlin Working Group for Coptic Gnostic Writings. The numbering of the verses within the sayings is according to the latter group.

5. For instance, see Matthew 23:6-7, 29-35 and Luke 11:43-51, a group of sayings considered part of the Q strand.

6. For instance, see "Messianic Claimants of the First and Second Centuries" in Craig Evans (1992), pp. 239-252.

7. Matthew 12:43-45 and Luke 11:24-26.

8. This is usually wrongly transliterated in the KJV as *ephphatha*. The Syriac version has the correct form *eth* added to the root peṭaḥ (94).

9. Heaven: šemayā (55).

10. Faith: haimānuṭā (36).

11. Matthew 8:5-13 and Luke 7:1-10. A modified form of this story of "distant healing"—perhaps a different healing or this one combined with another—is found in John 4:46-53.

12. The earliest Jewish mystical text (first to sixth century CE), the *Sepher Yetzirah* (Book of Creation), proclaims, for instance: "Twenty-two Foundation letters: He engraved them, He carved them, He permuted them, He weighed them, He transformed them. And with them, He depicted all that was formed and all that would be formed." Aryeh Kaplan (1990), p. 100.

13. Far from being simply an obscure method of interpreting texts, limited to the esoteric temperament, the interpretive, or *midrashic*, approach is extremely relevant to modern life according to the modern Israeli writer and peace activist Shulamith Hareven (1995): "[T]he constant, never-ending midrash is one of the strongest and most important ways of overcoming the damage caused by static, sanctified myth. Perhaps one of the most important things we can impart through education is the sense that all of us are free when it comes to myth, that we all have the freedom of *midrash*, of interpretation, that myth in our hands is clay in the hands of the potter" (p. 26).

14. Islamic scholar Annemarie Schimmel comments on the profundity of Quranic interpretation attempted by Islamic mystics and served by the Arabic language itself: "[T]he mystics of Islam . . . knew that a deeper meaning lies behind the words of the text and that one has to penetrate to the true core. It may be an exaggeration that an early mystic supposedly knew 7,000 interpretations for each verse of the Koran, but the search for the never-ending meanings of the

Koran has continued through the ages" (1992), p. 48.

15. Sufi scholar Seyyed Hossain Nasr elaborates on this (1968), p. 95ff.
16. For instance, Genesis 1:27.
17. For instance, the *Ma'aseh Bereshit*, an early Jewish mystical text, purports to relate practices that some scholars feel were present in Palestine before the time of Jesus. See, for instance, Kanagaraj (1998), p. 179ff.
18. Beginning: from rīšā (3)
19. Word: melṭā (136).
20. An expanded translation of this passage with textual notes can be found in DW, pp. 31-35.

CHAPTER THREE: BREATH

1. An early version of this chapter, entitled "Holy Spirit and Holy Breath in the Aramaic Words of Jesus," was delivered as one of the keynote papers at the 21st Mystics and Scientists Conference, sponsored by the Scientific and Medical Network at the University of Warwick, Coventry, England, April 1998. Other elements are taken from a paper given in the Mysticism Group at the 1997 Annual Meeting of the American Academy of Religion. See Douglas-Klotz, (1997).
2. Spirit: ruḥā (120).
3. For instance, in an encyclopedic summary of the last half century of this dialogue, Ian Barbour (1990) wends his way toward a conclusion that science and religion find their most fruitful meeting place in the process philosophy of Alfred North Whitehead. Barbour proposes that theologians undertake a "process theology" based on Whitehead, which would allow them to reframe passages in scripture to be in dialogue with scientific theories like evolution and relativity.
4. For this line of argument, I am indebted to Sufi scholar Seyyed Hossain Nasr's early work on spiritual ecology (1968). pp. 99-100.
5. Worship: sɛḡeḏ (138).
6. Truth: šerārā (125).
7. For more on this, see Fabre D'Olivet's extensive discussion in *The Hebraic Language Restored* (1815), especially pp. 3-60.
8. Enemy: bɛ'eldɛḇāḇā (31).
9. Also Mark 3:28-29, Luke 12:10 and Thomas, Saying 44.
10. Sin: haṭāha (116). Blasphemy: gudāp̄ā (8). Forgive: šɛḇaq (42).
11. For instance, Wilhelm Reich, an early student of Freud, broke with his mentor over the issue of the importance of the body in therapy. Reich wrote that holding the breath, which he saw as an attempt to suppress feeling the divine and erotic life force flowing through one, not only created disharmony in the individual, but also in society at large. See his pivotal work *Function of the Orgasm* (1948),

pp. 333ff, 360.

12. Mourn: ebal (86). Comfort: baya (19).

13. Meek: maḵīḵā (84). Inherit: yireṯ (62). Earth: 'ar'ā (30).

14. This is called proprioceptive awareness. For instance, see E. Gindler (1926), F. Alexander (1932), G. Alexander (1985), and Brooks (1982). A famous story in somatic therapy concerns Elsa Gindler, a teacher of physical exercise in Germany in the 1920s. Gindler was diagnosed with fatal tuberculosis in one lung. By fine-tuning her body awareness, however, she taught herself to breathe solely in her healthy lung, thereby giving the diseased side a chance to heal. This was not simply labeled spontaneous healing by the medical establishment of the time, due to the fact that she thereafter taught many others the same techniques and started several schools of somatic therapy that still exist today. Brooks (1982), p. 229ff.

15. These practices, sometimes called *merkabah* mysticism, had many different elements, including attaining a vision of the divine "throne-chariot," similar to the visions of Ezekiel and Isaiah. For more on this, see first Gershom Scholem (1954). In relation to possible influences on the Gospels of John and Thomas see, respectively, Kanagaraj (1998), and Patterson and Robinson (1998).

CHAPTER FOUR: HOLINESS

1. Holy: qadash (57).

2. nitqadash shmakh: see (57) and (89).

3. Pray: šelā (103).

4. For instance, Yeshua cleanses the Jerusalem Temple of commerce, quoting the words of both Isaiah and Jeremiah: 'Does not scripture say: My house will be called a house of prayer for all peoples? But you have turned it into a bandits' den.' (Mark 11:17, paralled in Matthew 21:13 and Luke 19:46, with reference to Isaiah 56:7 and Jeremiah 7:11.)

5. A rendition of a longer part of the hymn to Ptah can be found in DW, pp. 81 86.

6. Closet: tawānā (17). Door: tar'ā (29). Secret: beḵesyā (112). Openly: begleyā (95).

7. Ask: šēlu (2). Be given, receive: netyahb (104). Seek: be'a (114). Find: 'eškah (40). Knock: qōshw (65). Open: peṯaḥ (94). For an expanded translation of the passage with these possibilities, see DW, pp. 193-196.

8. For instance, see the work of Heikki Räisänen (1997), pp. 187-203.

9. Räisänen (1997) approaches the notion of *midrash* when he notes: "In the process of selective and conscious reinterpretation biblical ideas and concepts may well turn into 'symbols' (which is a more elusive notion). 'Kingdom of God,' 'resurrection,' 'redemption,' 'Christ,' even 'God' may be thoroughly problematic as concepts or ideas, but they may still serve as evocative and challenging sym-

bols. Symbols, values and stories can be freely moulded and used by people in the light of their experience and their sense of reality and responsibility" (p. 202).

10. For an elaboration of this openly ecumenical interpretation, see Krister Stendahl (1984), p. 239ff.

11. I am: enā enā (59). Way: urḥā (133). Truth: šerārā (125). Life: ḥayē (72).

12. Except: 'ēla (34). If: 'en (60). By, through: b (124).

CHAPTER FIVE: FACES OF LIGHT

1. Name: šemā (89). Compare with *shmakh*, "your light or name," which we saw in chapter four. Instead of giving a separate word for "your," Aramaic adds the possessive meaning as a suffix.

2. The writer of 1 John expresses this in the question: "For he that loveth not his brother whom he hath seen, how can he love God whom he hath not seen?" 1 John 4:20.

3. Isaiah 6:3. An interpretive expansion of this can be found in DW, pp. 245-246.

4. 1 Corinthians 6:19.

5. We could compare and contrast this concept with that of "dream-time" in the Australian Aboriginal tradition.

6. An expanded translation of this part of the story appears in DW, pp. 20-21.

7. Light: nuhrā (73).

8. Luke 11:33-36, and Matthew 5:15 and 6:22-23. This is considered Q saying #42 by John Kloppenborg (1990, 1994) and others.

9. For a longer discussion of this cultural level of meaning, see Lamsa (1939), pp. 27-29.

10. Lamp: šerāgā (67). Lampstand: menārtā (68). Bushel: saṭā (13). Secret place: from bekesyā (112).

11. Eye: 'ainā (34). Single: pešīṭā (117). Body: paḡrā (11).

12. Evil: bīšā (33). Darkness: ḥešukā (24).

13. Unless: dalmā (127).

14. Harmless, innocent: tamīmā (63).

15. A medieval text of Jewish mysticism, the Zohar (meaning "radiant life"), compares an image of the three parts of a candle to the three aspects of the soul. See DW, p. 153.

CHAPTER SIX: THE REIGN OF UNITY

1. Reign, kingdom: malkuṭā (105). Hebrew form: mamlākā.

2. The Jewish biblical scholar Savina Treubal (1990) makes a case that Sarah was

actually the matriarch and guide of the Abrahamic clan and that later Jewish redactors obscured this fact.

3. Repent: tāb (106). A word with the same root appears later in Arabic as one of the sacred attributes of Allah recognized in the Sufi tradition: *Ya Tawab*, the Releasing or Relenting.

4. Near: qereb (91).

5. Jewish biblical scholar Geza Vermes (1993) also points out this focus on immediacy in Jesus' teaching: "In a religion animated by true eschatological zeal, time becomes focused on the present. . . . In a world in which the *now* is sacrosanct, all dawdling is banned" (p. 193).

6. Observation: neturtā (93).

7. Inside: legau (64). Within: men (135).

8. For a brief overview of this period, see Shaye J. D. Coyen (1988).

9. Soul-self: napšā (118).

10. Come: teete (18).

11. Persecute: redap (102). Righteousness: khenūta (107).

12. Convert: hepak (21). Child: talyā (15). Humble: mak (58). Great: rab (51).

13. Parable: matlā (97).

14. Lamsa (1939), pp. 160-4.

15. Mustard seed: hardelā (87).

16. Yeast: hemīrā (140).

17. In a slightly different context, Geza Vermes (1993), in his study of the Jewishness of Jesus, notes this emphasis on the queen-kingdom as coming from inside out. "Unlike the rabbis and the Essene teachers who insisted on both the letter and the spirit of the Law, Jesus marched in the footsteps of the great prophets of Israel in placing an almost exaggerated accent on the *inward aspects* and *root causes* of the religious action. . . . Instead of solemnly laying down directives for an orderly social, cultic and moral life within a community of the elect, he sought to perfect their inner spiritual persona" (p. 195, emphasis in original).

CHAPTER SEVEN: BETWEEN HEAVEN AND EARTH

1. Pass away: 'ābar (98). Word: meltā (136).

2. While this theme occurs in much of the classical Sufi literature, its most beautiful modern expression is in the writings of the Indian Sufi Hazrat Inayat Khan (1962). See pp. 115-130.

3. Law: nāmosā (70).

4. Will: sebyānā (134).

5. Bind: 'esar (6). Loose: šerā (74).

6. For instance, see Marcus Borg (1994), p. 96ff.

7. Luke 14:16-24, although there are also some parallels to the story related in Matthew 22.

8. Possessed (Hebrew): qanani.

9. From DW, pp. 123-124. Further translations from the Hebrew of the portions of Proverbs relating to Hokhmah can be found in DW, pp. 103-104, 140-142.

10. For instance, Nag Hammadi scholar Gilles Quispel (1975) relates the Thunder text to Hokhmah.

11. The translations from "Thunder, Perfect Mind" are also from DW. See pp. 107, 126.

12. For the relation of schizophrenia to a failure of the somatic "sixth sense," see psychologist Wilhelm Reich's *Character Analysis* (1949).

13. For instance, "For whoso findeth me findeth life" (Proverbs 8:35) and "Counsel is mine, and sound wisdom: I am understanding; I have strength" (Proverbs 8:14).

14. Bread: lahmā (12).

CHAPTER EIGHT: SOUL, SELF, AND LIFE

1. Matthew 22:34-40 and Mark 12:28-31. Luke 10:25-28 gives another version of the incident in which the questioner actually provides the answer, whereupon Jesus gives a definition of neighbor using the story of the Good Samaritan. The usual translations of Matthew's version leave out the word "strength" (or "life"), but the Aramaic Peshitta version includes this word, making it consistent with Mark's version. The first section of the answer is contained in Deuteronomy 6:5, the second in Leviticus 19:18.

2. Deuteronomy also uses the Hebrew equivalent, *nephesh*. Leviticus 19:18 uses a different construction in its commandment about the neighbor, preferring "as you."

3. Love: reḥem (78). Lord: mārē (75). Heart: lebā (54). Mind: re'yānā (85). Strength: ḥailā (122).

4. This older layer of the brain carries many gifts that we may have forgotten, or that may have been superceded by more modern reasoning faculties. See, for instance, the eloquent case studies of Oliver Sacks (1984) and (1995), among others.

5. Neighbor: qarībā (92).

6. Matthew 16:25-26, Mark 8:35-36, and Luke 9:24-25.

7. Lose: 'ebad (76). Save: ḥeyā (111).

8. Gospel: sebartā (50), from sabar. As a sacred phrase, this word becomes very important later in the Sufi tradition as one of the ninety-nine names of Sacred

Unity: *As-Sabur*.

9. Gain: yītar (45). Lose: ḥesar (77).

10. Eternity: 'ālmā (32).

11. The Sufis later used the root of this word in one of the ninety-nine Names of Unity (*Al 'Alim*), meaning knowledge of all worlds.

12. Begotten: yiḥidāyā (4). We might compare this with the frequent use of the word "solitary" in the Gospel of Thomas as noted in chapter two. Believe: 'eṭe'men (5). Perish: eḇaḏ (101).

13. Know: yiḏa' (66). Mystery: rāzā (88).

14. Outside: barāyā (96). Parable: maṯlā (97).

15. See: ḥezā (113). Hear: šema' (53). Understand: sakel (126).

16. Unless: dalmā (127). Convert: penā (22).

17. Forgive: šeḇaq (42). Sin: ḥaṭāha (116).

18. The word for sin is also used in Luke's version of the seventh line of the prayer Jesus gave, usually translated: "And forgive us our sins; for we also forgive every one that is indebted to us." For more on this, see the expanded translation from the Aramaic text in POC, p. 30ff.

CHAPTER NINE: THE PERFECT AND THE GOOD

1. Perfect: g'mar (100).

2. Father: 'aḇā (38).

3. As mentioned in the acknowledgments, for ecological information on first century CE Palestine, I am indebted to the work of the Jesus and Ecology Project, which is a collaborative effort of Dr. Joseph Grabill of Illinois State University-Normal, Deborah Oberg, and myself.

4. Good: ṭāḇa (48).

5. The word is used this way in Matthew 26:19.

6. Evil: bīšā (33).

7. Luke has a similar version in 6:43-44.

8. Matthew 13:3-8, Mark 4:3-8, and Luke 8:5-8. Jesus' commentary is at Matthew 13:18, Mark 4:14-20, and Luke 8:11-15.

9. Sow: zera' (119). Fall: nepal (37).

10. The same word is also used in the Genesis account of creation. See DW, pp. 98-102, 115-116.

11. Adversary: sāṭānā (1).

12. For instance, the same term in Hebrew (*satan*) is used in Numbers 22:22 to describe the angel of God who blocked the way of Balaam's donkey.

13. For an detailed reconstruction of the process by which "Satan" is demonized and identified with the enemy in early Christianity, see Elaine Pagels' *The His-*

tory of Satan (1995).

14. Bird: pārahtā (7).

15. Rock: šu'ā (108). Depth: umqā (25). Root: 'eqārā (109).

16. Thorn: kubā (123).

17. Most likely either darnel (*lolium temulentum*) or scabiens (*cephalaria syriaca*). See D. Darom, *Beautiful Plants of the Bible*.

18. Enemy: bε'eldεbābā (31).

19. The modern agricultural model known as permaculture is based on this idea of harmonious growth in relation to the ecosystem. See, for instance, Mollison (1991).

20. In the King James version the word translated "lawful" is the Aramaic šalīṭā (71) meaning with power, authority, or harmonious order. It is related by its first root to shalama, or peace. The word for "evil eye" uses a form of bīshā (33). In combination with "eye" ('aina, 35), it can also mean envious or jealous.

21. Some New Testament Greek texts do not include the "called . . . chosen" passage, but it is included in the Peshitta, as well as in the Byzantine Majority Greek text.

22. Last: 'hεrāyā (69). First: qadmāyā (41).

23. Many: sagiyā' (82). Few: zε'urā (39).

24. Call: q'rā (14). Choose: g'bā (16).

25. See DW, pp. 59-60, 74.

CHAPTER TEN: FACES OF LOVE

1. It is worth noting that the Gospel of John contains almost twice as many "love" words as the other three Gospels combined.

2. Vision: εlāwā (132).

3. Worthy: šεwā (139). Pray: šelā (103).

4. Master: mārē (83). Serve: pεlah (115). Hate: sεnā (52). Hold: yiqar (56). Despise: šāṭ (26). Mammon: māmonā (81).

5. The Greek text transliterates it as *mamonas*, and Greek New Testament dictionaries relate the root to Aramaic.

6. Love: hab (79).

7. Enemy: bε'eldεbabā (31).

8. Bless: bεreḵ (9). An Arabic form of this word later means blessing-magnetism in the Sufi tradition: *baraka*.

9. Curse: lāṭ (23).

10. Do: 'εbad (28). In the Sufi traditon, the Arabic form of the word joins together the images of service, worship, and the *hab* type of love in an important sacred phrase: *mahabud lillah*: the beloved servant of Unity.

11. Good: šapīra (49). In the Sufi tradition, the Arabic form of this word is used to invoke the name of Unity as divine healing: *Ash-Shafi*.
12. Despiteful: qeṭīrā (27). Use: debar (129). This word is related to the Hebrew word *dabar*, used frequently in the Jewish scriptures to refer to the divine Word of creation. Persecute: reḏap̄ (102).
13. Commandment: puqdānā (20). Friend: rāḥmā (43).
14. Will: ṣeḇyānā (134).
15. Matthew 26:42, Mark 14:36, and Luke 22:42.
16. Mark 1:40-41, with parallels at Matthew 8:2-3 and Luke 5: 12-13.
17. Matthew 22:3.
18. Find: 'eškaḥ (40).
19. A more complete rendition of the entire passage may be found in DW, pp. 193-195.
20. Matthew 8:10.
21. With a parallel in Luke 13:24.
22. Straight: qaṭīna (121). Gate: tar'ā (46).
23. Narrow: 'alīṣā (90). Way: urḥā (133). Few: zɛ'urā (39). Life: ḥayē (72).
24. See DW, pp. 208-211.

Chapter Eleven: Yeshua bar Alaha

1. More on this discussion can be found in Werner Kelber's *The Oral and the Written Gospel* (1997).
2. For a discussion of this approach in relation to a "hermeneutics of indeterminacy," see Douglas-Klotz (1999).
3. For further references, see for instance, "Jewish Christianity in Egypt" by A. F. J. Klijn in *The Roots of Egyptian Christianity*, edited by Birger A. Pearson and James E. Goehring (1992), as well as *Holy Women of the Syrian Orient* by Sebastian P. Brock and Susan Ashbrook (1987).
4. For an excellent discussion of this topic, see Harold Coward's *Sacred Word and Sacred Text: Scripture in World Religions* (1988).
5. For the more exacting details of the ongoing scholarly controversy about this expression, see Geza Vermes' "The Use of Bar Nasha/Bar Nash in Jewish Aramaic" in Black (1967), and Joseph Fitzmyer's "The New Testament Title "Son of Man" Philologically Considered" in his *A Wandering Aramean: Collected Aramaic Essays* (1979).
6. See Kanagaraj (1998).
7. Matthew 12:8 with parallels at Mark 2:28 and Luke 6:5.
8. Matthew 9:6 with parallels at Mark 2:10-11 and Luke 5:24.
9. Lamsa's *Gospel Light* (1939), pp. 148-149.

10. For more on early Christianity and "low Christology," see Finnish New Testament scholar Heikki Räisänen's *Marcion, Mohammed and the Mahatma* (1997), for instance, pp. 87-91.

11. In the usual translations, the word "make" εḇāḏā (80). Peace: šεlāmā (99).

12. For a more detailed interpretation, see POC, pp. 65-67.

13. Matthew 26:27-29, with parallels at Mark 14:23-25 and Luke 22:17-18, 20.

14. Blood: dεmā (10). Fruit: yaldā (44). Vine: gεp̄etā (131).

15. Israel is referred to as a vine in, for instance, Jeremiah 2:21 and Hosea 10:1. In addition, Holy Wisdom refers to herself as a vine in the Jewish wisdom text Sirach, or Ecclesiasticus, written in approximately the second century BCE. For instance, Sirach 24: 17, 19: "I am like a vine putting out graceful shoots, my blossoms bear the fruit of glory and wealth. Approach me, you who desire me, and take your fill of my fruits." This is reminiscent of the saying of Jesus in John 15:4-5.

16. Matthew 26:26, with parallels at Mark 14:22 and Luke 22:19.

17. Body: paḡrā (11). Aramaic also has another word for body (gušmā), which refers to the body as a contraction of breath-energy. This is the "wave" view of body, as opposed to the "particle" one. The Aramaic version has Jesus use this word only once, in reference to the perfume poured on his body by the woman with the alabaster jar (Matthew 26:12, Mark 14:8).

AFTERWORD

1. The field takes its name from the Greek God Hermes, who was the master of both words and healing. As the inventor of language, Hermes was called a trickster, a thief, and a bargainer. According to Socrates in Plato's *Cratylus*, all of these attributes have to do with the fact that Hermes creates through language, and that words have the ability to reveal as well as conceal: "Speech can signify all things, but it also turns things this way and that" (in Hoy, 1978, p.1).

2. See Douglas-Klotz (1999).

3. For recent discussions of this see Patterson and Robinson (1998), and Uro (1998).

4. See Parrinder (1995).

5. This and the following translations from the Arabic of the Quran are by the author.

Glossary

This is an interpretive glossary of primary English words and their Aramaic equivalents according to the Syriac Peshitta version of the Gospels. The meanings given for the Aramaic words have been drawn primarily from *A Compendious Syriac Dictionary*, edited by J. Payne Smith (1903) Oxford: Clarendon Press; *The Hebraic Tongue Restored*, by Fabre D'Olivet (1815), Nayan Louise Redfield, trans. (1921 edition republished 1991) York Beach, ME: Samuel Weiser; *The Concordance to the Peshitta Version of the Aramaic New Testament* (1985) New Knoxville, OH: American Christian Press; and *Lexical Tools to the Syriac New Testament*, by George Anton Kiraz (1994) Sheffield: JSOT Press/Sheffield Academic Press.

This glossary lists only basic forms of words touched upon in my translations and should not be considered a substitute for one of the dictionaries or lexicons above. The numbers in parentheses are keyed to those in the endnotes, which identify instances where the word is found in the text.

Adversary: sāṭānā (1). That which causes one to turn aside or go astray.

Ask: šēlu (2). Pray, interrogate; carries a sense of urgency.

Beginning: from rīšā (3). Head, point, tip, beginning. From the Semitic roots R and Sh, indicating an unfolding of heat, light, or fire.

Begotten: yiḥiḏāyā (4). Single, solitary, or united in all aspects of being.

Believe: 'ete'men (5). To have a sense of confidence, trust, or firmness that comes from a rooted place. Related to *amen*. See also "faith."

Bind: 'esar (6). To tie oneself to something; to engage or enmesh oneself in some aspect of material existence.

Bird: pāraḥtā (7). From a verb that means to fly about, flutter, squander, dissipate, or diffuse something.

Blasphemy: gudāp̄ā (8). Incision, irruption, or furrow; what cuts one off.

Bless: berek (9). To kneel or bow down. From its roots, it suggests the centralization or embodiment of a potential creative force.

Blood: demā (10). Juice, wine, sap, essence.

Body: paḡrā (11). Flesh, corpse, carcass; what loses heat over time; the physical part of a being, without breath.

Bread: laḥmā (12). Food for all aspects of an individual; understanding.

Bushel: saṭā (13). A dry measure scoop; any round enclosure.

Call: q'rā (14). To invoke or invite. Related to the old Hebrew *kara*, which suggests the image of engraving, hollowing out.

Child: ṭalyā (15). One still under the shelter of parents, or who is covered or veiled; any unmarried youth.

Choose: g'bā (16). To approve or gather.

Closet: tawānā (17). A space—physical, emotional, or spiritual. The root TW points to a symbol, sign, or story that reveals something else behind it.

Come: ṭeeṭe (18). (Intensive form): come-come.

Comfort: baya (19). To be united inside or returned from wandering; to see the face of what one hopes for.

Commandment: puqdānā (20). From the Aramaic pākad—to visit, inspect, inquire, or review regularly; also means to judge, depart, or bequeath. The roots indicate an alternating, pendulum-like movement that stirs the substance through which it passes.

Convert: hɛpak (21). To change, move, give back, or restore. The roots point to alternating movements, like opening and shutting, coming and going, or to a process that proceeds contrary to expectation.

Convert: pɛnā (22). To return, answer, give back, or cause to turn. Related to the word for face or the front or first appearance of something.

Curse: lāṭ (23). Also, to cover, hide, detach, or soil something. From the roots come ideas of envelopment, seclusion, hiding, and mystery.

Darkness: ḥešukā (24). Chaos, circling or swirling energy, compression.

Depth: umqā (25). From the verb meaning to dig, hollow out, or search.

Despise: šāṭ (26). To neglect or consider worthless; related to the Aramaic word for a whip or lash.

Despiteful: qeṭīrā (27). From a verb meaning to tie together, bind, knot, or bring together through force or out of necessity.

Do: 'ɛbad (28). To make or work; to subdue, subject, or restrain oneself or another.

Door: tar'ā (29). Related to pɛṭaḥ. See "open."

Earth: 'ar'ā (30). Nature, embodied reality, all individual forms.

Enemy: bɛ'eldɛbābā (31). One who falls out of rhythm. Also, an owner, or head of a family. Comes from a root verb that means to dispute, or to inquire in a hostile manner. Its roots refer to domination, power, or pride taken to excess, such that one swells outwardly from an inner void or lack.

Eternity: 'ālmā (32). See "world."

Evil: bīšā (33). Unripe, not fit for its intended purpose, not ready, out of rhythm.

Except: 'ēla (34). But, if only, unless, although. All express a condition that passes away, like the body. Consequently, it is related to the word for mourning the dead.

Eye: 'ainā (35). Appearance, face, the surface of something; look, view, opinion.

Faith: haimānuṭā (36). Confidence, firmness, or integrity of being. From the roots, this word indicates a connection of the sacred life force (I) through its many outer forms (MN) in a way that is rooted, yet constantly renewing and healing.

Fall: nεp̄al (37). Also, to change state by scattering if solid and distilling if liquid.

Father: 'aḇā (38). Parent, ancestor, or founder. Based on the root AB, which points to all movements that seek to complete themselves or find an end; also, the desire to have, that which bears fruit.

Few: zε'urā (39). From a verb that means to diminish, to become weakened by fear of the future, or to be hemmed in on all sides.

Find: 'eškah (40). To invent, discover, or recover. From its root (ASh), suggests an embodied form of sacred fire or heat, which regenerates nature each season.

First: qaḏmāyā (41). That which was before or has existed from the most ancient times.

Forgive: šεḇaq (42). To restore to its original state; loosen, let go, set free, omit.

Friend: rāḥmā (43). See "love."

Fruit: yalda (44). Offspring or birth.

Gain: yītar (45). To surpass, exceed, or have an abundance of something.

Gate: tar'ā (46). Door. See "open."

God: 'alāhā (47). Unity, Oneness, the Ultimate Power or Potential, the One without an Opposite. A combination of the ancient Semitic root AL or EL, indicating the extent of anything or movement toward an end, as well as the definite article; along with LA, that which moves toward no end; also the negation of anything, the word "no."

Good: ṭāḇa (48). Ripe, fit for a particular purpose, ready. Its root points to something that maintains its integrity and health (T) by inner growth in harmony with what surrounds it (B).

Good: šapīra (49). Beautiful, healthy, or well; related to the words for clarity, daybreak, and the first glimmer of light.

Gospel: sebartā (50). From sabar: to hope, consider, endure, be nourished, preach, declare. From its roots: the containment (SB) of a sacred fire (AR), which instead of burning out of control provides warmth and heat over a period of time.

Great: rab (51). To multiply or grow greatly. Its root (RB) suggests the movement of creation and propagation.

Hate: sɛnā (52). From a root verb meaning to strain away, filter, or clarify. Related through its root to the word for the moon.

Hear: šɛma' (53). Can also indicate an inner sound or mystical vibration. Related to "name."

Heart: lebā (54). Center of courage, intelligence, and feeling; the breast; the mind; the pith, marrow, center, or best part of anything.

Heaven: šɛmayā (55). Sky; figuratively, the height or furthest extent of anything. From the particle šem, deriving from the ancient Semitic root ShM—name, light, sound, vibration, atmosphere. The -aya ending indicates that it is without limit.

Hold: yiqar (56). To honor or make heavy with burdens or belongings.

Holy: qadash (57). From the two Semitic roots KD, the point or pivot upon which everything turns, and ASh, the image of a circle unfolding from a point with power and heat.

Humble: mak (58). See "meek."

I am: enā enā (59). Intensive form of "I"; the essence of individuality; the "I-I"; the "I inside the I"; figuratively, the "I am."

If: 'en (60). Provided that, that; expressing a sense of present or actual time, that is, what is existing now, not in archetypal time.

In: b (61). See "through."

Inherit: yiret (62). To receive strength, power, sustenance.

Innocent: tamīmā (63). Harmless, simple, complete, straightforward, sincere.

Inside: legau (64). Inside, inward, the belly or viscera of a being or community.

Knock: qōshw (65). To pitch (a tent), strike (a note). Like the word for "holy," the root points to a hollowing out or inner spaciousness that comes from sincerity.

Know: yiḏaʿ (66). To be able to handle something.

Lamp: šerāḡā (67). From the verb šeraḡreḡ, meaning to be illuminated, to imagine, to dream.

Lampstand: menārtā (68). From nuhrā. See "light."

Last: ʿherāyā (69). From a verb that means to tarry, delay, linger, or remain behind.

Law: nāmosā (70). From roots meaning anything of beauty which helps relieve or take away that which deprives a human being of strength.

Lawful: šalīṭā (71). With power, authority, or harmonious order. From the noun šulṭānā, from which the Arabic word *sultan* is derived.

Life: ḥayē (72). Life force, animal energy, or the primal energy that pervades the cosmos.

Light: nuhrā (73). Intelligence, clarity, illumination, elucidation.

Loose: šɛrā (74). Liberates. From its roots: the symbolic image of a circle opening up, or of the umbilical cord being severed after birth.

Lord: mārē (75). From its roots (M, AR): a quality of obvious power; the manifested light that attracts one's attention.

Lose: ʿeḇaḏ (76). To go astray, destroy, fall away, or fall into decay. From its roots the word points to a process of self-surrender that results from reaching the furthest extent of a particular development.

Lose: ḥesar (77). To lack, be in want of, or be incomplete.

Love: rḥem (78). From the old Hebrew word for "womb": compassion, warmth that can pour from the depths of oneself. The roots suggest the radiating forth of light and heat (RA) from an interior place (ChM).

Love: ḥaḇ (79). To kindle a fire from something easily set ablaze, like withered leaves or dry sticks; to grow or produce something slowly from an enclosure or from a secret place. Related to the old Hebrew *ahabah*. The Semitic roots refer symbolically to the image of grain, or the germ of a seed, whose outer material substance (CH) covers the ability to produce fruit (AB).

Make: ɛḇāḏā (80). Also, to plant; something done regularly and with commitment.

Mammon: māmonā (81). The roots point to a piling up of outer things or appearances (MM), which become the definition of one's self or life (N).

Many: sagiyāʿ (82). From a verb that means to increase, multiply, or make abundant.

Master: mārē (83). See "lord."

Meek: makīkā (84). Humble. The Semitic roots point to liquefaction, melting, bowing down, and the softening of something overly rigid.

Mind: reʻyānā (85). The grasping, instinctual intelligence.

Mourn: ebal (86). To be in confusion or turmoil; to wander.

Mustard Seed: ḥardɛlā (87). From the roots AR and D, meaning something spreading freely, like a wildfire.

Mystery: rāzā (88). Any secret, a mystical signification, symbol, or sign. The roots convey the idea of extreme thinness or even the disappearance of something material; also, interior movement or sound.

Name: šɛmā (89). Light, sound, vibration, atmosphere.

Narrow: ʻalīṣā (90). Afflicted. From a verb meaning to compel, constrain, press, or make urgent.

Near: qereb (91). From a verb meaning to come, offer, arrive, seize, carry, or bring near; suggests proximity in time as well as space.

Neighbor: qarībā (92). One who is drawn near, or is in proximity. Can also be a member of the inner community of one's self.

Observation: neṭurtā (93). As a verb: to watch, guard, keep, preserve (including preserve in memory).

Open: pɛṭah (94). To open, increase, enlarge, spread widely.

Openly: begleyā (95). What is revealed by being manifested in form; figuratively, from the roots: the swell of the ocean as it builds slowly.

Outside: barāyā (96). From the word for open countryside or a wild area. Symbolically, from the roots B and AR, it is the radius defining the borders of a circle when viewed from the center, or the circumference of any area, or the fruit that is produced by the germ of a seed.

Parable: maṭlā (97). From mɛṭah: to stretch or extend something that can provide a cover over something else.

Pass away: ʻābār (98). To lose, cross over a boundary, go beyond, or exceed a limit.

Peace: šɛlāmā (99). From a verb that means to be fulfilled or complete, to surrender or be delivered, or to die.

Perfect: g'mar (100). As a verb: to accomplish, fulfill oneself, or be complete. A secondary meaning is to be completely consumed, cease, or disappear.

Perish: ebad (101). See "lose."

Persecute: reḍap̄ (102). To drive away, banish, dislocate, or dominate. Related by root family to the verb meaning to journey, flow, or continue.

Pray: šelā (103). To bend toward, incline, listen to; to lay a snare for. From the Semitic roots: figuratively, a bottomless depth; a shadow or shade created by a canopy or veil.

Receive: netyahb (104). Bearing fruit of a love that grows steadily from within. See also "father."

Reign, kingdom: malkuṭā (105): Queendom, counsel, ruling vision. The roots point to the creative word, the empowering vision, the counsel that rules by its ability to express the most obvious next step for a group. On a personal level, it is what says "I can!" to life.

Repent: tāḇ (106). Return, come again, flow back, ebb. The Semitic root TB suggests something that returns in a circle or spiral to its origins or its original rhythm.

Righteousness: khenūṭa (107). The base of justice; considering all parties equally.

Rock: šuʿā (108). From the verb meaning to stop up or obstruct something. Used metaphorically to mean closing the senses or heart.

Root: ʿeqārā (109). From a verb meaning to uproot or make something barren.

Sacrifice: debḥeṭā (110). From a verb meaning to slaughter or kill. From its roots: to separate something from its life essence.

Save: ḥeyā (111). To give life energy to. See "life."

Secret: bekesyā (112). Can also refer to inner sight. See "veil."

See: ḥezā (113). Also, to receive a vision quickly, in an instant.

Seek: beʿa (114). To search from the inside to the outside.

Serve: pelah (115). To labor, work, cultivate, plow, or meditate. The roots suggest images of emptying oneself, creating a channel through effort; movement from the outside in.

Sin: ḥaṭāha (116). Error, failure, mistake; what misses the mark; frustrated hopes; figuratively, tangled threads. Derives from the verbs meaning to dig out or sew— both having to do with an effort (CH) made against resistance (T).

Single: pešīṭā (117). Upright, stretched out, innocent, sincere, straightforward.

Soul-self: napšā (118). Soul, self, subconscious self.

Sow: zeraʿ (119). Scatter or spread abroad, generate or propagate. Related to the word for seed, a layered reality.

Spirit: ruḥā (120). Breath, wind, air. From the root, a raying forth (R) of life breath (H).

Straight: qaṭīna (121). Thin, frail, subtle, delicate, keen, or ethereal.

Strength: ḥailā (122). See "life."

Thorn: kubā (123). From a verb that means to feel pain or sorrow. From its Semitic roots, it points to anything that arrests one's natural growth or holds one back.

Through: b (124). Through, in, among, with, along with, at, to, into, on, by, for, or because. What unites these various meanings is the action of something passing from interior to exterior, or from idea to form.

Truth: šerārā (125). Right or harmonious direction; that which liberates and opens possibilities, or is strong and vigorous.

Understand: sakel (126). From a root meaning the end or limit of things, an enclosure, or a cover. Figuratively, it is a sack or package that both protects and hides something.

Unless: dalmā (127). It may be, except, perhaps. This word points out a condition or special circumstance in relation to something that has gone before.

Until: εdamā (128). So far, so that. Related to the verb meaning to touch, pass near, or come upon someone suddenly.

Use: dεbar (129). To lead, take, rule, or guide; related to the Hebrew word *dabar,* used frequently in the Jewish scriptures to refer to the divine Word of creation.

Veil: kesa (130). Also, to protect.

Vine: gεp̄etā (131). From a verb meaning to dig or form a body from; metaphorically, can be used in Hebrew or Aramaic to refer to blood lineage.

Vision: εlāwā (132). Also, awakening.

Way: 'urḥā (133). Path; the light that reveals a path or shows a hidden possibility. See "light."

Will: ṣebyānā (134). Desire, delight, consent; an inner agreement that leads to manifestation. From its roots, also points to things that swell or rise, come into harmony, and then move together like a large crowd, or a host of stars.

Within: men (135). Within, from, out of, at, on, or by. The sphere of activity of a process, or the image and definition of something; its mien, in older English usage.

Word: melṭā (136). Command, sentence, story; anything fully formed that runs from beginning to end.

World: ālmā (137). Eternity, age, generation, era. Based on a root that means youth or newness, everything that constantly arises in diversity in the worlds of form.

Worship: sɛḡeḏ (138). To bow, surrender, adore.

Worthy: šɛwā (139). Equal, or in equilibrium with. From a verb meaning to spread a table, make a bed, or level something that was uneven.

Yeast: ḥɛmīrā (140). Leaven. From the roots M and AR: something that glows within and spreads heat outwards.

BIBLIOGRAPHY

PRIMARY TEXTS AND RESEARCH TOOLS

The Concordance to the Peshitta Version of the Aramaic New Testament (1985). New Knoxville, OH: American Christian Press.

Greek New Testament (Nestle-Aland, 27th Edition, second printing) (1995). Gramcord Institute (electronic edition). (1993). Stuttgart: Deutsche Bibelgesellschaft.

A Hebrew and English Lexicon of the Old Testament (Abridged). (1997). Based on *A Hebrew and English Lexicon of the Old Testament* by F. Brown, S. R. Driver, and C. A. Briggs. Oxford: Clarendon Press, 1907. Digitized and abridged as a part of the Princeton Theological Seminary Hebrew Lexicon Project under the direction of Dr. J. M. Roberts. Vancouver, WA: Grammcord Institute.

Hebrew Masoretic Text. (1994). Westminster Hebrew Morphology. Philadelphia, PA: Westminster Theological Seminary. Electronic Edition. Vancouver, WA: Grammcord Institute.

Syriac New Testament and Psalms. Based on the 1901 Oxford: Clarendon Press edition prepared by G.H. Gwilliam. Istanbul: Bible Society in Turkey.

Peshitta Syriac Bible. (1979). Syrian Patriarchate of Antioch and All the East. London: United Bible Societies.

Ali, Yusuf A., trans. (1938). *The Holy Quran: Text, Translation, Commentary*. Lahore: Sh. Muhammad Ashraf.

Cowan, J. Milton and Hans Wehr, eds. (1976). *A Dictionary of Modern Written Arabic*. Ithaca, NY: Spoken Language Services, Inc.

D'Olivet, Fabre. (1815). *The Hebraic Tongue Restored*. Nayan Louise Redfield, trans. 1921 edition republished 1991. York Beach, ME: Samuel Weiser.

Errico, Rocco A. and Michael J. Bazzi. (1989). *Classical Aramaic, Assyrian-Chaldean Dialect, Elementary Book I*. Irvine, CA: Noohra Foundation.

Elliger, K. and W. Rudolph, eds. (1966/67) *Biblia Hebraica Stuttgartensia*. Stuttgart: Deutsche Bibelgesellschaft.

Falla, Terry C. (1991). *A Key to the Peshitta Gospels*. Volume 1: *Aleph-Dalath*. Leiden: E.J. Brill.

Guillaumont, A and H. Puech, G. Quispel, W. Till and Y. Al Masih, trans. (1959). *The Gospel According to Thomas*. New York: Harper and Row.

Jennings, William. (1979). *Lexicon to the Syriac New Testament*. Knoxville, OH: American Christian Press.

Kiraz, George Anton. (1994). *Lexical Tools to the Syriac New Testament*. Sheffield: JSOT Press/Sheffield Academic Press.

Kutscher, E. Y. (1976). *Studies in Galilean Aramaic*. Ramat Gan: Bar-Ilan University.

Lamsa, George M. (1957). *The New Testament from the Ancient Eastern Text*. San Francisco: Harper & Row.

Lipinski, Edward. (1997). *Semitic Languages: Outline of a Comparative Grammar*. Leuven: Peeters.

Robinson, Theodore H. (1962). *Paradigms and Exercises in Syriac Grammar*. Oxford: Clarendon Press.

Smith, J. Payne, ed. (1903). *A Compendious Syriac Dictionary*. Oxford: Clarendon Press.

Sokoloff, Michael. (1990). *A Dictionary of Jewish Palestinian Aramaic of the Byzantine Period*. Ramat-Gan, Israel: Bar Ilan University Press.

Thomas, Robert L., ed. (1981). *New American Standard Exhaustive Concordance of the Bible: Hebrew-Aramaic Dictionary*. Electronic Edition. Vancouver, WA: Grammcord Institute.

—————. (1981). *New American Standard Exhaustive Concordance of the Bible: Greek Dictionary*. Electronic Edition. Vancouver, WA: Grammcord Institute.

Whish, Henry F. (1883). *Clavis Syriaca: A Key to the Ancient Syriac Version Called "Peshitta" of the Four Holy Gospels*. London: George Bell & Sons.

BIBLICAL AND RELIGIOUS STUDIES

Armstrong, Karen. (1993). *A History of God*. New York: Ballantine Books.

Barbour, Ian J. (1990). *Religion in an Age of Science*. London: SCM Press.

Black, Matthew. (1961). *The Scrolls and Christian Origins: Studies in the Jewish Background of the New Testament*. Chico, CA: Scholars Press.

—————. (1967). *An Aramaic Approach to the Gospels and Acts.* Oxford: Clarendon Press.

Boman, Thorlief. (1960). *Hebrew Thought Compared with Greek.* Philadelphia: Westminster.

Borg, Marcus J. (1994). *Meeting Jesus Again for the First Time.* San Francisco: HarperSanFrancisco.

Brock, Sebastian. (1973). Early Syrian Asceticism. *Numen* XX, Fasc. I. Leiden: E. J. Brill.

—————. (1975). St. Issac of Ninevah and Syriac spirituality. *Sobornost* 7 (2).

—————. (1987). The priesthood of the baptised: Some Syriac perspectives. *Sobornost/Eastern Churches Review* 9 (2).

Brock, Sebastian P. and Susan Ashbrook Harvey. (1987). *Holy Women of the Syrian Orient.* Berkeley and Los Angeles: University of California Press.

Buber, Martin and Franz Rosenzweig. (1994). *Scripture and Translation.* Bloomington: Indiana University Press.

Coward, Harold. (1988). *Sacred Word and Sacred Text: Scripture in World Religions.* Maryknoll, NY: Orbis Books.

Coyen, Shaye J. D. (1988). Roman Domination. In H. Shanks, ed., *Ancient Israel: A Short History from Abraham to the Roman Destruction of the Temple.* Washington, DC: Biblical Archeology Society.

Crossan, John Dominic. (1994a). *Jesus: A Revolutionary Biography.* San Francisco: Harper SanFrancisco.

—————. (1994b). *The Essential Jesus.* San Francisco: HarperSanFrancisco.

Darom, David. (undated). *Beautiful Plants of the Bible: From the Hyssop to the Mighty Cedar Trees.* Herzlia: Palphot Ltd.

Dewey, Joanna. (1994). Textuality in an oral culture: A survey of the Pauline tradition. *Semeia* 65, 37-65.

Douglas-Klotz, Neil. (1990). *Prayers of the Cosmos: Meditations on the Aramaic Words of Jesus.* San Francisco: HarperSanFrancisco.

—————. (1995). *Desert Wisdom: The Middle Eastern Tradition from the Goddess through the Sufis.* San Francisco: HarperSanFrancisco.

—————. (1997). The natural breath. Toward further dialogue between Western somatic and Eastern spiritual approaches to the body awareness of breathing. *Religious Studies and Theology* 16 (2), 64-79.

—————. (1999). Midrash and postmodern inquiry: suggestions toward a hermeneutics of indeterminacy. *Currents in Biblical Studies* 7, (in press).

Elliot, J. K. (1996). *The Apocryphal Jesus.* Oxford: Oxford University Press.

Evans, Craig. (1992). *Noncanonical Writings and New Testament Interpretation.* Peabody, MA: Hendrickson Publishers.

Fine, Lawrence. (1992). The unwritten Torah. *Parabola* 17 (3), 65-70.

Fitzmyer, Joseph. (1974). *Essays on the Semitic Background of the New Testament.* Chico, CA: Scholars Press.

—————. (1979). *A Wandering Aramean: Collected Aramaic Essays.* Chico, CA: Scholars Press.

—————. (1997). *The Semitic Background of the New Testament.* (Combined edition of the two above books with new introduction). Grand Rapids, MI: Eerdmans and Livonia, MI: Dove Booksellers.

Fox, Matthew. (1986). *Original Blessing.* Santa Fe: Bear and Company.

—————. (1987.) *The Coming of the Cosmic Christ.* San Francisco: HarperSanFrancisco.

Graves, Robert and Raphael Patai. (1983). *Hebrew Myths: The Book of Genesis.* New York: Greenwich House.

Hareven, Shulamith. 1995. *The Vocabulary of Peace: Life, Culture, and Politics in the Middle East.* San Francisco: Mercury House.

Hornung, Erik. (1982). John Baines, trans. *Conceptions of God in Ancient Egypt: the One and the Many.* Ithaca, NY: Cornell University Press.

Janowitz, Naomi. (1989). *The Poetics of Ascent: Theories of Language in a Rabbinic Ascent Text.* Albany, NY: State University of New York Press.

Johnson, Luke Timothy. (1998). *Religious Experience in Earliest Christianity: A Missing Dimension in New Testament Studies.* Minneapolis: Fortress Press.

Kanagaraj, Jey J. (1998). *"Mysticism" in the Gospel of John.* Journal for the Study of the New Testament Supplement Series 158. Sheffield: Sheffield Academic Press.

Kaplan, Aryeh. (1990). *Sefer Yetzirah: The Book of Creation in Theory and Practice.* York Beach, ME: Samuel Weiser.

Kelber, Werner H. (1997). *The Oral and the Written Gospel: The Hermeneutics of Speaking and Writing in the Synoptic Tradition, Mark, Paul, and Q.* Bloomington: Indiana University Press.

Khan, Hazrat Inayat. (1962). Music. In *The Sufi Message*, Volume 2. London: Barrie & Jenkins.

Kloppenborg, John S. (1987). *The Formation of Q: Trajectories in Ancient Wisdom Collections.* Philadelphia: Fortress Press.

—————————. (1988). *Q Parallels: Synopsis, Critical Notes and Concordance.* Sonoma, CA: Polebridge Press.

Küng, Hans. (1993). *Christianity and World Religions: Paths of Dialogue with Islam, Hinduism, and Buddhism.* Maryknoll, NY: Orbis.

Lamsa, George M. (1933). *The Holy Bible from Ancient Eastern Manuscripts.* Philadelphia: A. J. Holman.

—————————. (1939). *Gospel Light: Comments on the Teachings of Jesus from Aramaic and Unchanged Eastern Customs.* Philadelphia: A. J. Holman.

—————————. (1979). *New Testament Origin.* San Antonio: Aramaic Bible Center.

Lategan, Bernard C. (1985). Reference: reception, redescription, and reality. In B. Lategan and W. Vorster, eds. *Text and Reality: Aspects of Reference in Biblical Texts.* Atlanta: Scholars Press.

Lee, Bernard J. (1988). *The Galilean Jewishness of Jesus.* Mahwah, NJ: Paulist Press.

Muzafferiddin, Al-Hajj Shaikh and Shems Friedlander. (1978). *Ninety-Nine Names of Allah.* New York: Harper and Row.

Nasr, Seyyed Hossain. (1968). *Man and Nature: The Spiritual Crisis in Modern Man* London: Unwin.

Nolan, Albert. (1992). *Jesus before Christianity.* London: Darton, Longman & Todd.

Neusner, Jacob. (1987). *What is Midrash.* Philadelphia: Fortress Press.

—————————. (1989). *Invitation to Midrash.* San Francisco: Harper & Row.

Nurbakhsh, Javad. (1983). *Jesus in the Eyes of the Sufis.* London: Khaniqahi-Nimatulallahi Publications.

Page, Charles R. II. (1995). *Jesus and the Land*. Nashville: Abingdon Press.

Pagels, Elaine. (1979). *The Gnostic Gospels*. New York: Random House.

——————. (1988). *Adam, Eve, and the Serpent*. New York: Random House.

——————. (1995). *The Origin of Satan*. New York: Random House.

Parrinder, Geoffrey. (1995). *Jesus in the Quran*. Oxford: Oneworld Publications.

Patterson, Stephen J. and James M. Robinson, Hans-Gebhard Bethage et al. (1998). *The Fifth Gospel: The Gospel of Thomas Comes of Age*. Harrisburg, PA: Trinity Press International.

Pearson, Birger A. and James E. Goehring, eds. (1992). *The Roots of Egyptian Christianity*. Philadelphia: Fortress Press.

Peters, F. E. (1990). *Judaism, Christianity and Islam: The Classical Texts and Their Interpretation*. Volume 3: *The Works of the Spirit*. Princeton, NJ: Princeton University Press.

Pilch, John J. (1998). No Jews or Christians in the Bible. *Explorations* 12 (2), 3.

Pixner, Bargil. (1992). *With Jesus through Galilee According to the Fifth Gospel*. Rosh Pina, Israel: Corazin.

Powelson, Mark and Ray Riegert, eds. (1996). *The Lost Gospel Q: The Original Sayings of Jesus*. Berkeley, CA: Ulysses Press.

Pritchard, James B. (1955). *Ancient Near Eastern Texts Relating to the Old Testament*. Second Edition. New Jersey: Princeton University Press.

Quispel, Gilles. (1975). Jewish gnosis and Mandaean gnosticism. In J.-E. Menard, ed., *Les Textes de Nag Hammadi: Colloque du Centre d'Histoire des Religions* (Strassbourg, 23-25 Octobre 1974), NHS 7, Leiden: E. J. Brill, 82-122.

Räisänen, Heikki. (1997). *Marcion, Muhammad and the Mahatma: Exegetical Perspectives on the Encounter of Cultures and Faiths*. London: SCM Press.

Rihbany, Abraham. (1916). *The Syrian Christ*. Boston: Houghton Mifflin.

Robinson, James, ed. (1978). *The Nag Hammadi Library in English*. San Francisco: HarperSanFrancisco.

Salibi, Kamal. (1998). *Who Was Jesus: A Conspiracy in Jerusalem*. London: I. B. Tauris.

Schimmel, Annemarie. (1992). *Islam: An Introduction*. Albany: State University of

New York Press.

Scholem, Gershom G. (1949). *Zohar, The Book of Splendor*. New York: Schocken Books.

——————. (1954). *Major Trends in Jewish Mysticism*. Third Edition. New York: Schocken Books.

Shanks, Herschel, ed. (1988). *Ancient Israel: A Short History from Abraham to the Roman Destruction of the Temple*. Washington, DC: Biblical Archeology Society

Stendahl, Krister. (1984). *Meanings: The Bible as Document and Guide*. Philadelphia: Augsburg Fortress.

Stern, David. (1996). *Midrash and Theory: Ancient Jewish Exegesis and Contemporary Literary Studies*. Evanston, IL: Northwestern University Press.

Torrey, C. C. (1933). *The Four Gospels*. New York: Harper and Row.

——————. (1936). *Our Translated Gospels*. New York: Harper and Row.

Treubal, Savina. (1990). *Hagar the Egyptian: The Lost Tradition of the Matriarchs*. San Francisco: HarperSanFrancisco.

Uro, Risto, ed. (1998). *Thomas at the Crossroads: Essays on the Gospel of Thomas*. Edinburgh: T. & T. Clark.

Vermes, Geza. (1981). *Jesus the Jew*. Philadelphia: Fortress Press.

——————. (1983). *Jesus and the World of Judaism*. Philadelphia: Fortress Press.

——————. (1993). *The Religion of Jesus the Jew*. Minneapolis: Fortress Press.

Wilson, B. E. (1997). The two notebook hypothesis: An explanation of seven synoptic patterns. *The Expository Times*, 108 (June), 265-268.

Cultural Studies, Hermeneutics, and Somatic Psychology

Alexander, F. M. (1932). *The Use of the Self*. New York: E.P. Dutton.

Alexander, Gerda. (1985). *Eutony: The Holistic Discovery of the Total Person*. New York: Felix Morrow.

Berman, Morris. (1989). *Coming to Our Senses: Body and Spirit in the Hidden History of the West*. New York: Simon and Schuster.

Berry, Thomas. (1988). *The Dream of the Earth*. San Francisco: Sierra Club Books.

Brooks, Charles V. W. (1982*). Sensory Awareness: The Rediscovery of Experiencing*. Santa Barbara, CA: Ross-Erikson.

Elul, Jacques. (1985). *The Humiliation of the Word*. Joyce Main Hanks, trans. Grand Rapids, MI: Eerdmans.

Feldenkrais, Moshe. (1977). *The Case of Nora*. New York, Harper & Row.

Gadamer, H. G. (1975). *Truth and Method*. New York: Seabury Press.

Gindler, Elsa. (1926). Gymnastik for Working People. An unpublished translation of "Die Gymnastik des Berufsmenschen" in *Gymnastik*, the journal of the German Gymnastik Foundation.

Hanna, Thomas. (1979). *The Body of Life*. New York: Alfred A. Knopf.

Hoy, David. (1978). *The Critical Circle: Literature, History and Philosophical Hermeneutics*. Berkeley: University of California Press.

Johnson, Don. (1984). *Body*. Boston: Beacon Press.

Juhan, Deane. (1987). *Job's Body*. Barrytown, NY: Station Hill Press.

Kockerlmans, J. (1975). Toward an interpretive or hermeneutic social science. *Graduate Faculty Philosophy Journal* 5 (1), 73-96.

Lings, Martin. (1992). The synthesis of language. *Parabola* 17 (3), 13-18.

Mollison, Bill. (1991). *Introduction to Permaculture*. Tyalgum: Tagari Publications.

Ormiston, Gayle L. and Alan D. Schrift, eds. (1990). *The Hermeneutic Tradition: From Ast to Ricoeur*. Albany, NY: State University of New York Press.

Ormiston, Gayle L. and Alan D. Schrift, eds. (1990). *Transforming the Hermeneutic Context: From Nietzsche to Nancy*. Albany, NY: State University of New York Press.

Rowan, John and P. Reason. (1981). *Human Inquiry: A Sourcebook of New Paradigm Research*. Chichester: John Wiley & Sons.

Reich, Wilhelm. (1948). *The Function of the Orgasm*. New York: Simon & Schuster.

————. (1949). *Character Analysis*. New York: Farrar, Straus and Giroux.

————————. (1983). *Children of the Future*. New York: Farrar, Straus and Giroux.

Sacks, Oliver. (1984). *A Leg to Stand On*. New York: Summit Books.

————————. (1995). *An Anthropologist on Mars: Seven Paradoxical Tales*. London: Picador.

The **Abwoon Study Circle** offers books, recordings, and information about retreats and workshops that support the work in this book. It can be contacted: in the USA at PO Box 361655, Milpitas, CA 95036-1655, email: 73523.3177@compuserve.com; in the United Kingdom via The Green House, 45 The Roman Way, Glastonbury BA6 8AB, England, email: 100273.117@compuserve.com; in Germany via email: 100265.3226@compuserve.com. It can also be contacted worldwide via its Internet website—http://www.abwoon.com—which posts a continually updated list of events and publications.

INDEX TO BIBLICAL PASSAGES

GENERAL INDEX

In this index, English words as they appear in the familiar King James Version are entered in quotation marks. The pages following these entries give the original meaning as translated from Aramaic or another primary source. Transliterated Aramaic/Hebrew words are entered in italics. An "n." following a page number indicates that the reference will be found in the notes.

To find discussion of specific passages, please refer to the preceding Index to Biblical Passages.

A

abba, 130

Aborigines, Australian, 74 n.5

Abwoon, 20-21, 66, 130, 148

Adam, 162, 165-166

adam, 36, 96, 165, 166

agape, 147

agathos, 132

agriculture, 94, 131, 136, 138-139

ahabah/hab, 147-148, 151, 152-153

Alaha, 14, 27-31, 56, 65. *See also* Sacred Unity; unity

alchemy, 143

Allah, 28

'alma, 122

amen, 122

"among," 18, 86, 87-88

angels, words/letters and, 35

animals, 108-109

aor, 75, 76, 164. *See also nuhra*

apocalyptic, 88-89

apprenticeship, 72

Arabic, 18, 35

ar'ah, 50, 100, 134

Aramaic, 5-6, 7, 8, 16, 19, 35; prepositions 18, 65, 86, 125; transliterations of 9. *See also individual words*

ascension, 52

"ask," 63

attunement, 71-72

B

babies, 70

Babylonian, 35

balance, 72, 105, 107, 144-145

bar, 149, 163-164

bar nasha, 163-164, 169

Barbour, Ian, 42 n.3

basileia, 84

Beatitudes, the, 48-50, 90-91, 144, 150, 165; *Prayers of the Cosmos* and, 7. *See also entries in Index to Biblical Passages*

"beginning," 37, 74, 107. *See also* creation

"begotten," 122

belief(s), 6, 64, 134. *See also* faith

"believe," 122

believers/non-believers, 134

berek, 149

bereshit mysticism, 173. *See also b'rishit/ b'reshith*

betzallem, 36

"bind," 103-105

"bird," 135-136

birds, 108-109

bisha, 132-133

"blasphemy," 45

"bless," 149

"blessed," 48

"blood," 166, 167

"body," 79, 167-168, 167 n.17

body awareness, 8-9, 32, 50, 73. *See also*

By the Same Author:

Desert Wisdom:

The Middle Eastern Tradition from the Goddess

through the Sufis

◆

Prayers of the Cosmos:

Meditations on the Aramaic Words of Jesus

◆

Sufi Vision and Initiation

QUEST BOOKS
are published by
The Theosophical Society in America
Wheaton, Illinois 60189-0270,
a worldwide, nonprofit membership organization
that promotes fellowship among all peoples of the world,
encourages the study of religion, philosophy, and science,
and supports spiritual growth and healing.

Today humanity is on the verge of becoming, for the first time in its history, a global community. The only question is what kind of community it will be. Quest Books strives to fulfill the purpose of the Theosophical Society to act as a leavening; to introduce into humanity a large-mindedness, a freedom from bias, an understanding of the values of the East and West; and to point the way to human development as a means of service, both for the individual and for the whole of humankind.

For more information about Quest Books,
visit **www.questbooks.net**
For more information about the Theosophical Society,
visit **www.theosophical.org**,
or contact **Olcott@theosmail.net**,
or (630) 668-1571.

The Theosophical Publishing House is aided by
the generous support of the Kern Foundation,
a trust dedicated to Theosophical education.